COVENANT

OTHER BOOKS BY JOHN WALTON . . .

Ancient Israelite Literature in Its Cultural Context
Bible Study Commentary: Obadiah, Jonah
    (with Bryan E. Beyer)
Chronological and Background Charts of the Old Testament
A Survey of the Old Testament (with Andrew E. Hill)

GOD'S
PURPOSE

♦

COVENANT

♦

GOD'S
PLAN

JOHN H. WALTON

ZondervanPublishingHouse
Academic and Professional Books
Grand Rapids, Michigan

A Division of HarperCollinsPublishers

Requests for information should be addressed to:
Academic and Professional Books
Zondervan Publishing House
Grand Rapids, Michigan 49530

Edited by Jan Ortiz
Cover design by Jody Langley
Cover photo copyright © W. Cody/Westlight

Library of Congress Cataloging-in-Publication Data
Walton, John H., 1952–
     Covenant : God's purpose, God's plan / John H. Walton.
         p.   cm.
     Includes bibliographical references and index.
     ISBN 0-310-57751-9 (paper)
     1. Covenants—Religious aspects—Christianity. I. Title.
BT155.W24   1994   93-45488
231.7′6—dc20   CIP

Printed in the United States of America

94 95 96 97 98 99 / CH / 6 5 4 3 2 1

To my students, whose questions always
stimulate reflection
and often necessitate reformulation.
May their tribe increase.

CONTENTS

ABBREVIATIONS

BAR   *Biblical Archaeology Review*
BASOR *Bulletin of the American Society of Oriental Research*
BBR   *Bulletin for Biblical Research*
CAD   *Chicago Assyrian Dictionary*, ed. A. L. Oppenheim et al. (Chicago: 1956–)
CBQ   *Catholic Biblical Quarterly*
GKC   Genesius–Kautzsch–Cowley. Genesius' *Hebrew Grammar* (Oxford: 1910)
HUCA *Hebrew Union College Annual*
JAOS   *Journal of the American Oriental Society*
JBL   *Journal of Biblical Literature*
JCS   *Journal of Cuneiform Studies*
JETS   *Journal of the Evangelical Theological Society*
JSNT   *Journal for the Study of the New Testament*
JSOT   *Journal for the Study of the Old Testament*
TB   *Tyndale Bulletin*
TDNT   *Theological Dictionary of the New Testament*, ed. Kittel and Friedrich (Eerdmans)
TDOT   *Theological Dictionary of the Old Testament*, ed. Botterweck and Ringgren (Eerdmans)
TJ   *Trinity Journal*
VT   *Vetus Testamentum*
UF   *Ugarit–Forschungen*
WTJ   *Westminster Theological Journal*
ZA   *Zeitschrift für Assyriologie*
ZAW   *Zeitschrift für die Alttestamentliche Wissenschaft*

ACKNOWLEDGMENTS

I would like to thank the administration of the Moody Bible Institute for the provision of a sabbatical during which time much of this book was put together. I am also grateful to the administration of Trinity Evangelical Divinity School for the opportunity to teach a seminar course, *Law as a Hermeneutical Problem*, which allowed me to research and formulate chapter ten. Finally, I must express my gratitude to my student, Peter Maris, who persisted in asking the penetrating questions that motivated me to the formulation of this proposal. I would also like to thank my student assistant, Bethany Fegley, for help in preparing the index.

INTRODUCTION

THE IMPORTANCE OF THE COVENANT
IN THE OLD TESTAMENT

If there is a single most important theological structure in the Old Testament, few would disagree that it must be the covenant. Israel's identity, history, and faith are as bound to the covenant as is America's to freedom and democracy. Both the Old and New Testaments weave their theology on the loom of history with the thread of the covenant. It is no wonder, then, that many of our theological systems are built around particular perspectives of the covenant. From the modern controversies surrounding the systematic frameworks of covenant theology and dispensationalism, to the theologies of promise, liberation, or theonomy, the covenant is one of the central issues. The discipline of biblical theology is not to be left out as its proponents struggle with the absence of covenant in wisdom literature, the absence of a prophetic view of the covenant, or the absence of a redemptive pattern of the covenant. Critical scholarship is concerned with the development of the theology of the covenant in Israelite religion and how the various traditions (e.g., priestly or deuteronomic) contributed to the idea of the covenant.[1] Exegetes debate the etymology of the terms and the details of each passage that offers pertinent information. Specialists in comparative studies explore the similarities between the biblical covenant format and the format of first and second millennium international treaties.

THE CONTROVERSY ABOUT THE COVENANT

One would think that by now controversies regarding the covenant would be exhausted. But an issue of this magnitude can never finally be laid to rest. Many scholars have addressed the history of the covenant. Others have investigated the results or consequences, ramifications or implications.

Further controversy revolves around differences of opinion as to the number of covenants, their purpose, their function, their conditionality or unconditionality, and their fulfillment. These issues along with many other aspects of covenant have given definition to some of the entrenched factions within Protestantism. Denominations have been and continue to be built on perspectives of the covenant and their implications. Two of the major tracks of evangelicalism, "covenant theology" and "dispensationalism" have disparate views of the covenant at the core of their dispute with one another.

But controversy aside, the most basic area of study is to be found in studying the purpose of the covenant. What is the purpose of the covenant? Why did God make promises to Abraham, Moses, David, indeed, to Israel? Were promises made simply for the sake of making promises in order to keep them? Was the covenant inherently a redemptive program? Was it an extension of God's suzerainty over his people?

Although much has been written on the covenant, the camp is still divided and no resolution has been offered that has succeeded in developing a consensus with regard to this important concept. There is, therefore, room for yet another attempt to study the covenant and to improve our understanding of it. In this book it is suggested that the path toward an evangelical consensus is not to be found in the building of another modified systematic theology. Rather, the resolution of differences is more likely to be found in a biblical-theology approach. The perspective of the covenant that is proposed in this book is a model of the biblical-theology approach. It is hoped that this model will promote a better understanding of both the Israelites and the Bible and, in the end, will help us achieve a fuller knowledge of God. In this sense it is my hope to follow in the path of a number of recent evangelical scholars who have been calling for such an approach.[2]

NOTES

[1]For a convenient summary of critical scholarship's treatment of the covenant see E. W. Nicholson, *God and His People* (Oxford: Clarendon Press, 1986).

[2]Particularly Walter C. Kaiser in his numerous contributions to theological discourse as well as Kenneth Barker, "False Dichotomies Between the Testaments" *JETS* 25 (1982): 3–17 (esp. p. 15); see also K. Barker "The Scope and Center of Old and New Testament Theology and Hope," in *Dispensationalism, Israel and the Church*, ed. C. A. Blaising and Darrell K. Bock (Grand Rapids: Zondervan, 1992), 293–328.

1

THE PURPOSE
OF THE COVENANT

COVENANTS IN THE ANCIENT NEAR EAST

Before embarking on a study of the biblical material, it is appropriate to discuss to what extent the ancient Near East is able to provide information that offers a contemporary cultural understanding of the covenant idea.

In Akkadian, the language of Babylon and Assyria, the terms *mamitu* and *adu* have been identified as being pertinent to the discussion of the covenant. The first term, *mamitu*, refers to an oath or a sworn agreement.[1] While these oaths are typically sworn in the name of deity, they are not descriptive of agreements between God and man.[2] The second term, *adu*, refers to a formal agreement, and is therefore more likely to overlap with the Old Testament concept of covenant.[3] An *adu* is often finalized with a *mamitu*.

The term *adu* has been recognized as a loanword from Aramaic.

> The agreement called *adu* was drawn up in writing between a partner of higher status (god, king, member of the royal family) and servants or subjects. It was typically made secure by magic and also by religious means (ceremonies, curses, and oaths).[4]

Simo Parpola has suggested five distinct denotations for it:
- Solemn promises made by God to a king,
- A sworn agreement between gods,
- A peace treaty between two great kings,
- An agreement between a great king and lesser kings sought by the latter, and
- Conspiracy.[5]

Category one is of most interest for the present study, but Parpola offers only one example, and it is not a convincing one. Since neither of these terms is a cognate to the Hebrew term for covenant, and since neither represents agreements between God and man involving promises and election, I conclude that the extant literature of the ancient Near East offers no direct parallels to the covenant of the Old Testament.[6]

THE MEANING OF *BERIT*

The Hebrew term for covenant is *berit*. Although a number of suggestions have been proffered for the etymology of the word, the two most common derivations are from Akkadian, *birit* (between, among) and Akkadian, *biritu* (clasp, fetter).[7] In accordance with modern linguistic sensitivity, however, we must agree that etymology does little to contribute to our understanding of *berit*. The very fact that the cognate languages do not use a cognate term for similar concepts should warn us against making too much of an etymology, even if we were more certain of what the etymology is. The synchronic approach, preferred by today's scholars, insists that the lexical parameters of the word be defined in accordance with its usage.

In the Old Testament the term *berit* is used to refer to international treaties (Josh. 9:6; 1 Kings 15:19), clan alliances (Gen. 14:13), personal agreements (Gen. 31:44), legal contracts (Jer. 34:8–10), and loyalty agreements (1 Sam. 20:14–17) including marriage agreements (Mal. 2:14). In other words, on any level of society, a promise to do something would be formalized by means of a *berit*.

> Covenant in the normal secular practice of the ancient world appears to have been a device whereby existing relationships

which time, circumstances, or other factors have brought
into being, were given the semblance of legal backing in the
form of a ceremony whose major thrust was that of solemn
commitment.[8]

In this book, however, I am not as interested in discussing what
a covenant is, as I am in discussing why a covenant was made.
The former has little demonstrable impact on the latter.

DIFFERING VIEWS ON THE FUNCTION-PURPOSE OF THE COVENANT

Neither diachronic nor synchronic lexical analysis of the
word *berit* provides an understanding of the purpose or
function of the covenant that God made with Israel. All that can
be said is that God entered into a covenant with Israel as a
means of formalizing the promises he had made to Abraham
and the agreement he had made with Israel. Questions remain,
however. *Why* did God make these promises to Abraham? *Why*
did God choose an elect people for himself? What was his
purpose for taking a promise-covenant course of action? In
attempting to answer these questions, it is essential to differentiate between purpose and function. There may be many
different functions of the covenant, but if they are incidental or
secondary, they may have little to do with the purpose of the
covenant. Over the years many different positions have
emerged that reflect on the significance of the covenant, not all
of them mutually exclusive. Each will be examined in terms of
its ability to explain the purpose of the covenant.

Covenant as Promise

Many have viewed the covenant as a vehicle by which the
promise of God is formalized, defined, and protected. The
promise itself is defined as the "eternal expression of God's
will," and the "instrument that obligates God to act on behalf of
his people."[9] In this view, "The primary function of the
promise covenant is to grant the inheritance."[10] Interpreters
such as Willis J. Beecher and Walter Kaiser have identified the
promise as being the center of Old Testament theology and

have likewise seen the covenants as simply giving shape and expression to the promise.[11] The promise itself, then, concerns God's intention to bless, and more specifically, his intention to provide salvation.

Covenant as Grace, Redemption, or *Heilsgeschichte*

Evangelical theologies have consistently viewed redemption as being the focal point of all of the Bible. Classical dispensationalism attempted to balance covenant theology by focusing on the larger issue of the glory of God[12] yet still affirming the fullness of the redemptive program. Nonetheless, it is very difficult to detect any difference in recent literature between dispensationalists and covenant theologians with regard to the thrust of the covenant(s): God's purpose is to redeem and bless his people, with the ultimate intent of bringing glory to himself.

While it would be difficult to disagree that this has been God's ultimate purpose since Creation, one experiences substantially more difficulty in establishing it as the purpose of the covenant. Neither the Abrahamic nor the Davidic covenants suggest anything of any kind of redemption. The covenant of Sinai speaks of God's deliverance of Israel from slavery, but no comparison is made between that deliverance and salvation from sin until the New Testament. The new covenant comes the closest to a discussion of redemption in the mention of forgiveness of sin. But in the Old Testament this forgiveness is not identified as either redemption or salvation, thus raising the question of whether such a concept was understood as central to the covenant idea.

It is important at this point to make some very necessary observations with regard to terminology. The term *redemption* is used extensively in theological literature, but is used for two significantly disparate ideas: God's deliverance of Israel from Egypt, Babylon, and other oppressors is referred to as God's redemptive activity. Likewise God's provision of personal salvation from sin is considered to be redemptive. Thus the term *redemption* is used to bind together issues that have little in common except for the attribute of God that brings them about.

Semantic imprecision is thereby used to provide a foundation for theological systematization. In the discussion of this book, the word *redemption* will be defined as the provision of physical deliverance by God and will be used only in that sense. To describe a provision of salvation for sins I will use the term *soteric*. It is problematic to identify either a soteric or redemptive purpose for the covenant when the Old Testament covenants make so little of them (though certainly the new covenant lays the foundation for the development of the soteric element). Typically the reason theologians, when dealing with covenants, draw out the redemptive elements is so they can build to the soteric element.

The main thrust behind this emphasis on the soteric can be traced back to Johannes Cocceius in the seventeenth century.

> The prominence [Cocceius] gave to the idea of the redemptive activity of God in history and his choice of the covenant as the center point of his entire discussion correspond to some of the most characteristic emphases of the Old Testament. It is a tribute to his insight that these two themes have continued to play a role in the subsequent treatment of Old Testament theology, for we shall meet his definition of biblical religion in terms of a *history of redemption* or, to use the German word, of a *Heilsgeschichte*, again and again, and in his selection of the covenant idea he was a forerunner of a dominant approach in nineteenth- and twentieth-century scholarship.[13]

The emphasis on redemption in its larger sense continues to be reflected in the writings of contemporary covenant theologians as well, as Edward J. Young clearly expresses.

> Old Testament theology is concerned with the study of genuine revelation that the true God gave to Israel. These revelations had to do with His purposes in the salvation of mankind. His plan of salvation may be subsumed under the word covenant. It is, therefore, with the covenant of grace that Old Testament theology is concerned. This is its true content; this is its true subject matter.[14]

More recently, O. Palmer Robertson expressed similar opinions:

> Covenant theology understands the whole of history after man's fall into sin as unifying under the provisions of the covenant of redemption (or more traditionally, the covenant of grace). Beginning with the first promise to Adam-in-sin and continuing throughout history to the consummation of the ages, God orders all things in view of his singular purpose of redeeming people to himself.[15]

Others such as William J. Dumbrell, though distancing themselves from the classical form of covenant theology, likewise affirm that the covenant is properly viewed as a redemptive program. So he observes, "We must not lose sight of the fact that the call of Abraham in this passage is a redemptive response to the human dilemma which the spread of the sin narratives of Genesis 3–11 have posed."[16] He concludes that "the Kingdom of God established in global terms is the goal of the Abrahamic Covenant."[17]

These are examples from what is known as covenant theology, and they give central place to what is termed the *covenant of grace*.[18] This understanding of the covenant, as already mentioned, is not too far removed from that which was also being reflected in nonconservative circles.

Critical scholars use the term *heilsgeschichte* when they refer to documents concerning Israel's perspective on history or how they interpreted their history, in contrast to documents preserving a record of what actually happened. This view understands theology as being a recital of the redemptive acts of God in history. Another major distinction between this view and that of covenant theology is that the critics are not interested in connecting the saving acts of God with salvation from sin. Despite these differences in terminology and presupposition, the resulting view links covenant and "saving history" very closely in the editing of the Pentateuchal sources. As a result, Gerhard von Rad concludes that:

> the two covenants which Jahweh made, the one with Abraham and the other on Sinai with Moses, are what lay

down the lines of the whole work of JE. In it, contrary to
what is normal in matters cultic, everything is attuned to
events that are unique, and occur at the very beginning. The
covenant with Abraham and the covenant with Moses are
now connected with one another and with the whole course
of the saving history from Genesis to Joshua.[19]

These same views are reflected in postwar statements
emerging from the World Council of Churches.

> As to "Biblical Theology," then, there was wide agreement
> that a more or less unified message runs through the Bible,
> centering in *Heilsgeschichte* or the history of the divine-human
> covenant in its various forms and phrases.[20]

Covenant as Administrative or Relational

Some interpreters see the covenant as being God's initia-
tive in establishing a relationship with his elect people, and as
serving as the means by which that relationship is adminis-
tered. A few examples will demonstrate how this is articulated.
Theodorus Vriezen states:

> By concluding the Covenant with Israel Yahweh enters into
> communion with this people. The Hebrew word *berith*
> (covenant) means something like "bond of communion"; by
> concluding a covenant a connective link is effected (by means
> of a sacrifice or a meal or both) between the two partners,
> who thereby enter into an intimate relationship.[21]

William Most says:

> Since he could not want a covenant for gain to himself, it
> must be that He made it out of spontaneous, unmerited,
> generous love. But we may still ask why that love decided to
> use a covenant form. At least two reasons seem obvious: 1)
> Human beings in general are apt to mistrust God, saying: His
> ways are above ours as the heavens are above the earth: Who
> can understand them? Israel in particular came from a milieu
> in which the gods were objects of mistrust. A covenant could
> be a device of love to make men know where they stand, to
> reassure them that at least under specified conditions they
> may have confidence. 2) His spontaneous love wants to give
> favors to men.[22]

Similar positions are expressed by Ronald Clements and Gerhard von Rad.[23]

The purpose of election is certainly relational,[24] but that does not mean that the purpose of the covenant is relational. The goal of God's plan is relationship, but there are objectives along the way that have their own sub-purposes. Likewise, there is no doubt that one of the functions of the covenant is relational. But the fact that the covenant has a purpose beyond that relationship with Israel is evidenced in the contexts in which God carries on the program "for his own name's sake," not because of Israel or his relationship with them. Some of these passages will be explored more carefully below.

Covenant as Vassal Treaty and/or Land Grant

In addition to the now well-known correlation of the covenant with ancient Near Eastern treaties,[25] it has also been recognized that the covenants of the Bible are not homogeneous. Rather, they equate to two related but separate forms of corporate agreements; treaties (obligation) and land grants (promise).[26]

> While the "treaty" constitutes an obligation of the vassal to his master, the suzerain, the "grant" constitutes an obligation of the master to his servant. In the "grant" the curse is directed towards the one who will violate the rights of the king's vassal, while in the treaty the curse is directed towards the vassal who will violate the rights of his king. In other words, the "grant" serves mainly to protect the rights of the *servant*, while the treaty comes to protect the rights of the *master*. What is more, while the grant is a reward for loyalty and good deeds already performed, the treaty is an inducement for future loyalty.[27]

In addition to the differences between the two, there are important similarities as well.

> There certainly is a functional and formal overlap between these two types of documents. While the grant is mainly a promise by the donor to the recipient, it presupposes the loyalty of the latter. By the same token the treaty, whose

principal concern is with the obligation of the vassal, presupposes the sovereign's promise to protect his vassal's country and dynasty. This close similarity of treaty and grant is most clearly demonstrated in the Hittite treaty, which is based on the suzerain's bestowal of land to his vassal. It is met with likewise in the covenant of Deuteronomy, whose introduction also combines the gift of the land to the Patriarchs with the covenant between God and the people.[28]

While it is clear that the covenants of the Old Testament are formulated in accordance with the stylistic customs of ancient Near Eastern practice, the discipline of comparative studies has taught us well that form does not always dictate function. For instance, though the formulation of laws in the Pentateuch has much in common with the formulation of ancient Near Eastern laws, the function of those laws is quite distinct. Likewise the fact that the form of the covenants compares well with the forms of documents in the ancient Near East does not mean that function or purpose is shared.

On one hand, as indicated above by Weinfeld, the purpose of the ancient Near Eastern treaties and land grants was to induce loyalty and to reward loyalty respectively. On the other hand, how helpful would the analogy of foreign relations have been for Israel's understanding of her relationship to God? Nicholson touches on some of the problems.

> Vassals did not as a rule "love" those who conquered, subdued, and dominated them—there is abundant evidence for this in the history of Israel and of the ancient Near East— and the very language of intimate and familial relationships employed in the treaties reflects not the reality of the relationships, but rather the political, strategic, and economically motivated endeavor of suzerains to maintain, with the least amount of trouble, the subservience of those whom they had conquered and regarded as subject to them. To tell Israelites that Yahweh "loves" them in the same way as a suzerain (e.g., Ashurbanipal or Nebuchadrezzar) "loves" his vassals, and that they are to "love" Yahweh as vassals "love" their suzerains, would surely have been a bizarre depiction of Yahweh's love of, and commitment to, his people, and of

the love and commitment with which they were called upon to respond.[29]

No one would argue that loyalty was not important to the LORD.[30] Loyalty is necessary for the relationship that God seeks to establish with his creatures. Therefore, ultimately, the covenant can be seen as one of the mechanisms God is using in his overall plan. But his plan is not satisfied in relationships with Abraham, Israel, or the Davidic house. Those covenants and those relationships cannot be an end in themselves, but must be seen as a means to a more comprehensive end. This is how these covenants differed functionally from their ancient Near Eastern counterparts.

NOTES

[1]CAD M/1:189.

[2]The Tukulti-Ninurta Epic apparently uses *mamitu* in such a way, but the context is too broken to allow for more information, cf., CAD M/1:190.

[3]CAD A/1:131.

[4]Ibid., 133. M. Weinfeld surveys the Akkadian terminology in "Covenant Terminology in the Ancient Near East and Its Influence on the West" *JAOS* 93 (1973): 190–99.

[5]S. Parpola, "Neo-Assyrian Treaties from the Royal Archives of Nineveh" *JCS* 39 (1987): 181–82.

[6]M. Weinfeld, *"berith"* TDOT 2:278.

[7]Ibid., 253–55. For support of *birit* see R. Youngblood, "The Abrahamic Covenant: Conditional or Unconditional" in *The Living and Active Word of God* ed. M. Inch and R. Youngblood (Winona Lake: Eisenbrauns, 1983), 34. For support of *biritu* see K. Kitchen, "Egypt, Ugarit, Qatna and Covenant" *UF* 11 (1979): 453–64; W. Dumbrell, *Covenant and Creation* (Nashville: Nelson, 1984), 16; F. Cross, *Canaanite Myth and Hebrew Epic* (Cambridge: Harvard University Press, 1973), 268. For detailed analysis of the options see E. W. Nicholson, *God and His People* (Oxford: Clarendon Press, 1986), 89–109.

[8]W. J. Dumbrell, *Covenant and Creation*, 19.

[9]T. McComiskey, *The Covenants of Promise* (Grand Rapids: Baker, 1985), 72–73, 140.

[10]Ibid., 144.

[11]W. J. Beecher, *The Prophets and the Promise* (1905; reprint, Grand Rapids: Baker, 1975); W. C. Kaiser, *Toward an Old Testament Theology* (Grand Rapids: Zondervan, 1978).

[12]Charles C. Ryrie, *Dispensationalism Today* (Chicago: Moody Press, 1965), 103–5.

[13]John H. Hayes and Frederick Prussner, *Old Testament Theology: Its History and Development* (Atlanta: John Knox, 1985), 22–23.

[14]Edward J. Young, *The Study of Old Testament Theology Today* (Westwood, N.J.: Revell, 1959), 84.

[15]O. Palmer Robertson, *The Christ of the Covenants* (Phillipsburg, N.J.: Presbyterian and Reformed, 1980), 206.

[16]W. J. Dumbrell, *Covenant and Creation* (Nashville: Nelson, 1984), 47.

[17]Ibid., 78.

[18] This term does not describe any particular biblical covenant, but is a theologically constructed composite of biblical covenants.

[19]G. von Rad, *Old Testament Theology* (New York: Harper and Row, 1962), I:133. J and E are two of the hypothetical pentateuchal sources combined by some into source JE.

[20]John Hayes and Frederick Prussner, *Old Testament Theology: Its History and Development* (Atlanta: John Knox, 1985), 212.

[21]Th. Vriezen, *An Outline of Old Testament Theology* (Oxford: Basil Blackwell, 1960), 168.

[22]W. G. Most, "The Biblical Theology of Redemption in a Covenant Framework" *CBQ* 29 (1967): 7.

[23]R. E. Clements, *Old Testament Theology: A Fresh Approach* (Atlanta: John Knox, 1978), 101; G. von Rad, *Old Testament Theology*, I:131.

[24]Seock-Tae Sohn, *The Divine Election of Israel* (Grand Rapids: Eerdmans, 1991), 195.

[25]For more detailed analyses of this approach see E. W. Nicholson, *God and His People*, 56–82; D. J. McCarthy, *Treaty and Covenant* (Rome: Biblical Institute Press, 1978), and also his *Old Testament Covenant* (Atlanta: John Knox, 1972).

[26]M. Weinfeld, "The Covenant of Grant in the Old Testament and in the Ancient Near East," *JAOS* 90 (1970): 184–203.

[27]Ibid., 185.

[28]M. Weinfeld, *Deuteronomy and the Deuteronomic School* (1972; reprint, Winona Lake: Eisenbrauns, 1992), 74.

[29]E. W. Nicholson, *God and His People*, 79.

[30]"In regard to the divine name *YHWH*, commonly referred to as the *Tetragrammaton*, the translators [of the NIV Bible] adopted a device used in most English versions of rendering that name as 'LORD,' in capital letters to distinguish it from *Adonai*, another Hebrew word rendered 'Lord,' for which small letters are used." *The NIV Study Bible* (Grand Rapids: Zondervan, 1985), xii.

2

A PROPOSAL: COVENANT AS GOD'S PROGRAM OF REVELATION

There are many aspects to the positions presented in chapter 1 that are appropriate and accurate. There is, however, a need for a new proposal regarding covenant. In laying out a new proposal it is not my intention to take a departure from all that has gone before. Instead, I have looked for the strengths of each view of covenant, so in a sense this proposal represents an integration. I am suggesting that the focus and purpose of the covenant are something that has been in nearly everyone's formulation of covenant all along, though it has not been in the forefront. My thesis is as follows:

> God has a plan in history that he is sovereignly executing. The goal of that plan is for him to be in relationship with the people whom he has created. It would be difficult for people to enter into a relationship with a God whom they do not know. If his nature were concealed, obscured, or distorted, an honest relationship would be impossible. In order to clear the way for this relationship, then, God has undertaken as a primary objective a program of self-revelation. He wants people to know him. The mechanism that drives this program is the covenant, and the instrument is Israel. The purpose of the covenant is to reveal God.

To see how this differs from the standard view of covenant theology we can compare the conclusions of O. Palmer Robertson:

What is the point of the covenant? It is to establish a oneness between God and his people. That oneness which was interrupted by the entrance of sin must be reconstituted through the covenant of redemption. "I shall be your God and you shall be my people," functioning as the central unifying theme of the covenant, underscores the role of oneness as the essence of the goal of the covenant.[1]

In Robertson's formulation the relationship element comes through very strongly as being God's overall goal, but no distinction is drawn between that goal and the particular objective of the covenant program. In overidentifying the goal with the objectives that contribute to the goal, covenant theology has been forced into trying to read a redemptive element into every phase of the covenant. The difficulty with this endeavor is that the text is not very cooperative. In contrast, my proposal, which has been suggested above, sees revelation as the particular *objective* of the covenant program. In the end, revelation culminates in God's plan of salvation, which provides the means by which relationship is achieved. But this plan of salvation is only one part, albeit a highly significant part, of the overall program of revelation. Those who understand the covenant as being redemptive (soteric) will at times attach revelation as a secondary element. Ned Stonehouse, for instance, states, "In thus graciously drawing near unto man for his salvation God makes himself known to man, and thus the covenant of grace is at one and the same time redemptive and revelatory."[2] From the perspective of progressive dispensationalism, R. L. Saucy eloquently addresses Israel's role as a channel of revelation yet sees the covenant as a "kingdom program of salvation."[3]

My proposal reverses these emphases. The covenant is revelatory and this program of revelation eventuates in redemption, or in, to make the distinction clear, salvation. My contention, then, is that while the covenant is characteristically redemptive, and ultimately soteric, it is essentially revelatory. Likewise, even though election in the new covenant is soteric in nature, and thus consummates in a relationship born through justification, election in the Old Testament is not so defined. As mentioned above, election establishes a relationship between God and the elect, but we must ask what the purpose of election is in each individual circumstance. Recently William W. Klein has suggested a purpose for the election of Israel with which I agree.

> God's love alone stands as the motive for his choice of the people of Israel to be his own. Never do the biblical writers describe election as a reward. It does not come in response to any attribute or action of Israel. His election did not give Israel a privileged position among the nations so she might gloat. Rather, God chose Israel to serve him and reflect his character and ways to other nations—"that they may proclaim [His] praise" (Isa. 43:21). In this sense God's election of Israel parallels his election of individuals—he has called her into existence to serve him in the world. Thus Israel's election does not mean God has rejected the other nations. Rather, election creates for Israel the task of representing God among the nations so salvation might come to them.[4]

Turning to the classical Old Testament theologies, Theodorus Vriezen and Walther Eichrodt are closer to this view than other interpreters. Vriezen places much emphasis on revelation, but is more concerned with the prophets as mediators of the revelation than with the covenant as its mechanism. Eichrodt, as is well known, posits the covenant as the center of the Old Testament, but does not dwell on the role that it plays within the program of revelation. He describes the covenant, on the one hand, as "a free act of God, consummated in history, [that] has raised Israel to the rank of the People of God, in whom the nature and will of God are to be revealed."[5] He continues,

> As an epitome of the dealings of God in history the "covenant" is not a doctrinal concept, with the help of which a complete corpus of dogma can be worked out, but the characteristic *description of a living process*, which was begun at a particular time and at a particular place, in order to reveal a divine reality unique in the whole history of religion.[6]

On the other hand, Eichrodt weaves many of the functions mentioned in the above survey of covenant into his analysis. He suggests a progressive shifting in the concept of covenant with D viewing it as a symbol for expressing religious relationship, and P restricting it to salvation history.[7] Furthermore he sees the revelation as pertaining primarily to saving acts.

> For P *berit* is the ideal term to express the concept of a religion of revelation, based entirely on God's promise and holding fast, in spite of the fact that time and place must necessarily limit its realization, to the universality of the divine saving plan.[8]

It also must be admitted that there is some overlap with George Ernest Wright's concept of theology as being the recital of the acts of God.

> Inferences are constantly made from the acts and are interpreted as integral parts of the acts themselves which furnish the clue to understanding not only of contemporary happenings but of those which subsequently occurred. The being and attributes of God are nowhere systematically presented but are inferences from events.[9]

Thus God's acts in history are understood by Wright as being the revelation of his will and purpose as well as of his nature, which is the aspect my proposed model emphasizes. The difference is that Wright does not merge the covenant into this picture in the same way.

Another contemporary theologian whose thoughts have some similarity to this position is Jakob Jocz who, like Eichrodt, chose the covenant as the organizing feature of his theology.[10] Again, however, his understanding of the covenant is largely in relational terms rather than in revelatory terms, and he most frequently identifies covenant with the condescension of God. The closest Jocz comes to the ideas expressed in my proposal is when he goes so far as to say that revelation takes place in the context of the covenant—in itself not an earth-shattering admission.[11] But even here he is describing revelation in terms of the covenant context rather than the covenant in terms of a program of revelation. Likewise Jocz accepts the *Heilsgeschichte* model, as can be seen in his summary statement concerning the covenant and revelation.

> It is our contention that revelation unless structured in the covenant is without anchorage and becomes a matter of speculation. Within the covenant context the biblical attributes cease to be philosophical concepts but become descriptions of God's saving acts within history. It is only in the covenant that we know Him, that He is for us and on behalf of us. In the last resort covenantal knowledge of God is Christologically conditioned. That God is truly for us and that the covenant still stands we can only know through Jesus Christ.[12]

As with many of the above statements, there is much here that I agree with and that can easily be adopted into the position here proposed.

Seock-Tae Sohn in his study of the divine election of Israel, views election as having, among other purposes, a revelatory purpose.

> Yahweh elected Israel to make himself known to the world through her. Israel was to show that "there is none like him in all the earth" (Ex. 8:10; 9:14; 14:4, 18), "the earth is Yahweh's" (9:29), and "Yahweh is greater than all the gods" (18:11). By doing miracles and wonders for Israel, Yahweh demonstrated his existence and power to Israel as well as to other foreign nations. Thus Yahweh used Israel to be an instrument, to be his witness.[13]

Sohn's view also shows some similarity to the hypothesis that I have proposed here in that election is a very significant aspect of the covenant.

Other theologians, among them Gerhard Hasel, Ronald E. Clements, and Robert Saucy, have mentioned this revelatory function in passing without really incorporating it into a larger view.

> God is shown as the God of the world and of Israel in that he bound himself to man and Israel in a special manner through election and covenant.[14]

In a very deep and inescapable fashion the belief that there is a special revelation of God in the Old Testament is related to the belief that he has chosen and used Israel in a special way to bring this knowledge to all mankind.[15]

The priestly ministry of Israel entailed that people as the avenue of God's saving revelation to the world. . . . Moreover, the verbal record is only one means of God's revelation; he also makes himself known through historical actions."[16]

CONCLUSION OF COMPARISON

In order to draw a concluding differentiation between the position that I have proposed and the classical evangelical positions, John Feinberg's definition of the major theological views is a good place to begin:

> For nondispensationalists, history is seen primarily as salvation history. In other words, the emphasis is on God's ongoing plan in saving men. For dispensationalists, history is the gradual implementation and outworking of the kingdom of God. A major part of that implementation involves saving people, but the soteriological and spiritual elements are not the only aspects of the kingdom.[17]

In my proposal both salvation and kingdom are important aspects of the covenant-revelation program, but neither is the primary focus. They are both subsumed under the aegis of an overarching plan of God's revealing his character, his will, and his plan. In so doing, God provides a foundation for relationship with him (knowing God and being like him), a means by which that relationship might be achieved (salvation), and the structure that will define that relationship (kingdom).

BIBLICAL SUPPORT OF THE REVELATORY PURPOSE

It is important at the outset to establish biblical support for the hypothesis that has been laid out above. As one might expect, scriptural evidence is not conclusive else the controversy would not have existed for so long. Nevertheless, there is sufficient proof so that one is able to proceed with this model as a working hypothesis, relying on detailed development to

provide further support both from Scripture and from logical
reasoning and deduction (as do all theological models).

One of the key elements for investigation is the frequently
recurring phrase "then you [they] will know that I am Yahweh"
and the numerous variations on that theme. Before moving on
to a study of biblical support passages, however, it is necessary
to discuss a more basic issue concerning whether this terminology stresses revelation or relationship.

A number of scholars who have studied the treaties of the
ancient Near East have concluded that the Hebrew word *yada'*,
to know, is paralleled in these treaties and carries a relational
meaning. So, for instance, Delbert Hillers concludes: "Thus,
verbs meaning 'to know' in ordinary contexts were used for 'to
recognize,' 'be loyal to,' in the vocabulary of international
relations over a wide range of the ancient world. . . ."[18]

Certainly this conclusion, on the one hand, offers support
for the idea that covenant and revelation are closely associated,
even in the terminology that is used (i.e., one enters a
relationship as a result of receiving information). On the other
hand, such conclusions present some difficulties by suggesting
the possibility that "knowing God" does not refer to revelation,
but to loyalty. Upon reflection, however, loyalty may be the
issue in contexts where the text uses God or Israel as the direct
object of the verb *yada'* (e.g., Hos. 13:4–5; Amos 3:2), but
cannot easily be inferred when a *ki* clause introduces a phrase
serving as the direct object (e.g., "then they will know *that* I am
the LORD").

The meaning "to recognize" suits well enough when the
direct object of the verb is a noun or pronoun (e.g., to *know*
Yahweh could mean to recognize Yahweh's suzerainty). It is
not as suitable when the direct object is a subordinate noun
clause (e.g., to know that I am Yahweh). If the subordinate
clause used a title connected to suzerainty (e.g., to know that
Yahweh is Lord of the earth), there would still be the possibility
that recognition of suzerainty was intended. The fact, however,
that these contexts use the personal name Yahweh makes such
an interpretation less likely (e.g., "to know that I am Yahweh,"
rather than "to know that I am God"). In contrast, when a

phrase such as "then all the earth may know that the LORD is God" (e.g., 1 Kings 8:60; 18:37; 2 Kings 5:15; 19:19), the meaning "to recognize" is acceptable. But even in these cases such recognition comes through a process of revelation. We would conclude then that the use of this phrase indicates at least a revelatory result or function, if not a revelatory purpose, for the actions described in the context.

Overall View of the Material

At the beginning of our investigation into the biblical support of my proposal (see p. 24), it is important to determine the range of possible situations that define the contexts in which God does something so that someone will know that he is the LORD. What actions does God perform and who is supposed to benefit from the resulting revelation? The chart on page 32 shows the distribution of the passages.

Specific Passages

There are a select number of these judgment-grace passages, as well as a few not listed here, that require particular attention. We will now look at these selected passage individually. The first ten passages show the revelatory nature of the covenant as it is part of God's election of the people of Israel.

Exodus 6:2–8

2God also said to Moses, 'I am the LORD. 3I appeared to Abraham, to Isaac and to Jacob as God Almighty, but by my name the LORD I did not make myself known to them. 4I also established my covenant with them to give them the land of Canaan, where they lived as aliens. 5Moreover, I have heard the groaning of the Israelites, whom the Egyptians are enslaving, and I have remembered my covenant.

6"Therefore, say to the Israelites: 'I am the LORD, and I will bring you out from under the yoke of the Egyptians. I will free you from being slaves to them, and I will redeem you with an outstretched arm and with mighty acts of judgment. 7I will take you as my own people, and I will be your God. Then you will know that I am the LORD your God, who brought you out from under the yoke of the Egyptians. 8And

Judgment against the nations so nations will know	Judgment against the nations so Israel will know	Judgment against Israel so Israel will know	Grace toward the nations so the nations will know	Grace toward Israel so the nations will know	Grace toward Israel so Israel will know
Ex 7:5	Ex 10:2	Isa 52:6	Ex 8:10	Jos 4:24	Ex 6:2-8
Ex 7:17	Eze 39:21-22	Jer 16:21	Ex 9:29	1Sa 17:47	Ex 16:6-12
Ex 9:14	Joel 3:14-17	Eze 6:7-14	Isa 45:3	Isa 49:26	Ex 29:46
Ex 14:4		Eze 7:4		Eze 36:22-23	Ex 31:13
Ex 14:18		Eze 7:27		Eze 37:24-28	Dt 4:32-40
1Sa 17:46		Eze 11:10-12		Eze 39:23-28	Dt 7:7-9
Eze 25:4-7		Eze 12:15-20			Dt 29:6
Eze 25:8-11		Eze 13:14			1Ki 20:13, 28
Eze 25:15-17		Eze 13:21-23			Ps 106:7-8
Eze 26:6		Eze 14:8			Isa 49:23
Eze 28:22		Eze 15:7			Isa 60:16
Eze 29:3-9		Eze 20:26			Eze 16:59-63
Eze 30:5-8		Eze 20:38			Eze 20:39-44
Eze 30:19		Eze 22:16			Eze 28:24-26
Eze 30:25-26		Eze 24:20-27			Eze 29:21
Eze 32:15		Eze 33:29			Eze 34:20-31
Eze 35:3-15					Eze 36:8-12
Eze 38:23					Eze 36:24-38
Eze 39:6-7					Eze 37:5-14
					Eze 39:25-29
					Joel 2:25-27

I will bring you to the land I swore with uplifted hand to give
to Abraham, to Isaac and to Jacob. I will give it to you as a
possession. I am the LORD.' "

This passage is the foundation passage for Israel's election
as the people of God. By bringing the Israelites into the land,
the LORD is here seen performing acts of deliverance and
fulfilling the promises made to the Patriarchs. The sequence is
that (1) when the LORD *delivers* Israel and *elects* them, then
(2) they will know (acknowledge)[19] that he is the LORD, and
then (3) he will *fulfill* his promise concerning the land. The
interpretation of what is meant by "then you will know that I
am the LORD" (v. 7) must be based on the contrasting statement
in verse three, where Moses is told that the name *Yahweh* was
not fully revealed to the Patriarchs.[20] Israel achieved its
knowledge of God through his acting on their behalf, by his
doing what he had promised he would do.

The element of slavery and deliverance is easily seen to be
related to God's promise of the land. God could not bring his
people into the land of promise without first bringing them out
of the land of slavery. Therefore God hears their groaning and
remembers his covenant; delivering them from slavery and
giving them the Promised Land. What is of particular interest in
this passage is that its very logical sequence is interrupted by
the election-revelation formula (i.e., You will be my people, I
will be your God, then you will know. . .), rather than the
formula coming at the conclusion of the passage. Certainly this
could be explained as a function of chronology (Exodus, Sinai,
conquest), but in any case the result is that the *knowing* aspect is
most readily connected with Sinai.

From this I infer that verse two suggests that the Patriarchs
had not benefited from a systematic revelation of the nature of
Yahweh as was made available to the people of Israel at Sinai
through the giving of the Law. That is what would be meant by
not making himself known as Yahweh, for in Genesis it is clear
that the name was familiar. God's past promises to Abraham,
his acts of deliverance from Egypt, and his eventual gift of the
land—all covenant items—are clarified and put into a revelato-

ry perspective through the election of Israel and the covenant agreement at Sinai.

If there is any element in these verses that can be identified as being the purpose for which God is electing Israel and entering into a covenant relationship with them, it is that as a direct result of God's actions, Israel would know that God was the LORD their God. This conclusion is also expressed by Garr.

> As a consequence of God's initiating the covenantal relation-
> ship, the human party will have knowledge or recognition,
> the object of which is the Israelite God (that he is Yahweh,
> their God). According to Exodus 6:7, knowing that Yahweh
> is God is a result of the covenantal relationship.[21]

I am suggesting, then, that the purpose of the covenant can be discerned by identifying what it was essential for. The covenant, on the one hand, was not essential for deliverance. God did not enter into a covenant with Israel in order to save them. On the other hand, the covenant *was* essential for revelation. Indeed, this text suggests that revelation would not have been accomplished in a clear way by the acts of deliverance alone. The covenant gave meaning and purpose to the acts of deliverance, therefore finding its purpose in revelation. Likewise, the text also offers evidence that God is not making a covenant so he can fulfill promises. The election-revelation formula precedes the fulfillment of the promises. Saving, electing, and fulfilling are all activities designed so that Israel will know that Yahweh is their God.

Deuteronomy 4:32–40

32 Ask now about the former days, long before your time,
from the day God created man on the earth; ask from one
end of the heavens to the other. Has anything so great as this
ever happened, or has anything like it ever been heard of?
33 Has any other people heard the voice of God speaking out
of fire, as you have, and lived? 34 Has any god ever tried to
take for himself one nation out of another nation, by testings,
by miraculous signs and wonders, by war, by a mighty hand
and an outstretched arm, or by great and awesome deeds,

like all the things the LORD your God did for you in Egypt
before your very eyes?

35 You were shown these things so that you might know
that the LORD is God; besides him there is no other. 36 From
heaven he made you hear his voice to discipline you. On
earth he showed you his great fire, and you heard his words
from out of the fire. 37 Because he loved your forefathers and
chose their descendants after them, he brought you out of
Egypt by his Presence and his great strength, 38 to drive out
before you nations greater and stronger than you and to
bring you into their land to give it to you for your
inheritance, as it is today.

39 Acknowledge and take to heart this day that the LORD is
God in heaven above and on the earth below. There is no
other. 40 Keep his decrees and commands, which I am giving
you today, so that it may go well with you and your children
after you and that you may live long in the land the LORD
your God gives you for all time.

As in the previous passage, here the elements of deliverance from Egypt, promises to the fathers, conquest of the land,
and, in more specific language, God's words from Sinai, have
as their purpose that "you" may know that Yahweh is God.

Deuteronomy 7:7–9

7 The LORD did not set his affection on you and choose you
because you were more numerous than other peoples, for
you were the fewest of all peoples. 8 But it was because the
LORD loved you and kept the oath he swore to your
forefathers that he brought you out with a mighty hand and
redeemed you from the land of slavery, from the power of
Pharaoh king of Egypt. 9 Know therefore that the LORD your
God is God; he is the faithful God, keeping his covenant of
love to a thousand generations of those who love him and
keep his commands.

Lest we should think of it the other way around, this
passage demonstrates that the election of Israel is a result of the
covenant. The covenant was not made so that Israel's election
could take place. Election is one of the means by which the
covenant achieves its purposes. Here the text makes it clear that

God chose Israel and redeemed Israel because of the covenant, with the expected result that they would "know that the LORD is God." Neither deliverance from slavery nor election as God's people are ends in themselves. They are means to an end, that end being identified here as revelation.

Psalm 106:7–8

7When our fathers were in Egypt,
they gave no thought to your miracles;
they did not remember your many kindnesses,
and they rebelled by the sea, the Red Sea.

8Yet he saved them for his name's sake,
to make his mighty power known.

Here the psalmist makes it clear that the immediate objective of Yahweh's acts of deliverance was not deliverance itself, but was revelation. Deliverance (redemption) is not the path to relationship here; revelation is. Furthermore, the reason his name was in jeopardy was that since Israel was his people his reputation was dependent on their conduct and success. It was understood that the covenant relationship created a revelatory situation. How Yahweh acted with his people revealed what he was capable of and what he was like.

2 Samuel 7:22–24

22How great you are, O Sovereign LORD! There is no one like you, and there is no God but you, as we have heard with our own ears. 23And who is like your people Israel—the one nation on earth that God went out to redeem as a people for himself, and to make a name for himself, and to perform great and awesome wonders by driving out nations and their gods from before your people, whom you redeemed from Egypt? 24You have established your people Israel as your very own forever, and you, O LORD, have become their God.

In this passage the revelatory purpose (God's making a name for himself) is listed alongside redemption and land possession. Just as the previous contexts demonstrated the continuity between Sinai and the promises to the Patriarchs, this passage understands the Davidic covenant in the context of both the promises to the Patriarchs (the land) and the deliverance from Egypt (Sinai).

Ezekiel 16:59–63

⁵⁹This is what the Sovereign Lord says: I will deal with you as you deserve, because you have despised my oath by breaking the covenant. ⁶⁰Yet I will remember the covenant I made with you in the days of your youth, and I will establish an everlasting covenant with you. ⁶¹Then you will remember your ways and be ashamed when you receive your sisters, both those who are older than you and those who are younger. I will give them to you as daughters, but not on the basis of my covenant with you. ⁶²So I will establish my covenant with you, and you will know that I am the Lord. ⁶³Then, when I make atonement for you for all you have done, you will remember and be ashamed and never again open your mouth because of your humiliation, declares the Sovereign Lord.

Ezekiel 16:59–63 is an important passage for two reasons. First, it relates a covenant of the future to a covenant of the past. Then it identifies at least the result, if not the purpose, of the future covenant as being God's revelation of himself.

Ezekiel 20:5–14, 19–22, 26, 38–44

⁵and say to them: "This is what the Sovereign Lord says: On the day I chose Israel, I swore with uplifted hand to the descendants of the house of Jacob and revealed myself to them in Egypt. With uplifted hand I said to them, 'I am the Lord your God.' ⁶On that day I swore to them that I would bring them out of Egypt into a land I had searched out for them, a land flowing with milk and honey, the most beautiful of all lands. ⁷And I said to them, 'Each of you, get rid of the vile images you have set your eyes on, and do not defile yourselves with the idols of Egypt. I am the Lord your God.'

⁸"But they rebelled against me and would not listen to me; they did not get rid of the vile images they had set their eyes on, nor did they forsake the idols of Egypt. So I said I would

pour out my wrath on them and spend my anger against them in Egypt. [9]But for the sake of my name I did what would keep it from being profaned in the eyes of the nations they lived among and in whose sight I had revealed myself to the Israelites by bringing them out of Egypt. [10]Therefore I led them out of Egypt and brought them into the desert. [11]I gave them my decrees and made known to them my laws, for the man who obeys them will live by them. [12]Also I gave them my Sabbaths as a sign between us, so they would know that I the LORD made them holy.

[13]"Yet the people of Israel rebelled against me in the desert. They did not follow my decrees but rejected my laws—although the man who obeys them will live by them—and they utterly desecrated my Sabbaths. So I said I would pour out my wrath on them and destroy them in the desert. [14]But for the sake of my name I did what would keep it from being profaned in the eyes of the nations in whose sight I had brought them out. [19]I am the LORD your God; follow my decrees and be careful to keep my laws. [20]Keep my Sabbaths holy, that they may be a sign between us. Then you will know that I am the LORD your God.

[21]" 'But the children rebelled against me: They did not follow my decrees, they were not careful to keep my laws— although the man who obeys them will live by them—and they desecrated my Sabbaths. So I said I would pour out my wrath on them and spend my anger against them in the desert. [22]But I withheld my hand, and for the sake of my name I did what would keep it from being profaned in the eyes of the nations in whose sight I had brought them out. [26]I let them become defiled through their gifts—the sacrifice of every firstborn—that I might fill them with horror so they would know that I am the LORD.'

[38]" 'I will purge you of those who revolt and rebel against me. Although I will bring them out of the land where they are living, yet they will not enter the land of Israel. Then you will know that I am the LORD.

[44]" 'You will know that I am the LORD, when I deal with you for my name's sake and not according to your evil ways and your corrupt practices, O house of Israel, declares the Sovereign LORD.' "

This lengthy recital in the context of Ezekiel 20:4–44 begins with Israel in Egypt and documents the long history of its rebellion. At each step Scripture identifies the LORD's actions as having been done "for my name's sake" (vv. 9, 14, 22, 44). Likewise, the recurring revelatory formula ("Then you will know that I am the LORD," vv. 7, 20, 26, 38, 44) shows that whether God's action in deliverance, judgment, covenant promises, or future restoration is the subject of the discussion, revelation is the expected result.

Ezekiel 34:22–31

22I will save my flock, and they will no longer be plundered. I will judge between one sheep and another. 23I will place over them one shepherd, my servant David, and he will tend them; he will tend them and be their shepherd. 24I the LORD will be their God, and my servant David will be prince among them. I the LORD have spoken.

25I will make a covenant of peace with them and rid the land of wild beasts so that they may live in the desert and sleep in the forests in safety. 26I will bless them and the places surrounding my hill. I will send down showers in season; there will be showers of blessing. 27The trees of the field will yield their fruit and the ground will yield its crops; the people will be secure in their land. They will know that I am the LORD, when I break the bars of their yoke and rescue them from the hands of those who enslaved them. 28They will no longer be plundered by the nations, nor will wild animals devour them. They will live in safety, and no one will make them afraid. 29I will provide for them a land renowned for its crops, and they will no longer be victims of famine in the land or bear the scorn of the nations. 30Then they will know that I, the LORD their God, am with them and that they, the house of Israel, are my people, declares the Sovereign LORD. 31You my sheep, the sheep of my pasture, are people, and I am your God, declares the Sovereign LORD.

The Davidic covenant, seen from the context of Ezekiel 34:20–31, is drawn together with other covenant issues (peace and safety in the land) and the restoration. Put in the context of the revelatory formula the Davidic covenant, the other cove-

nant issues, and the restoration are evidence that Israel is the
elect people of the LORD (v. 30).

Ezekiel 36:19–23, 26–28, 31–32, 36–38

¹⁹I dispersed them among the nations, and they were
scattered through the countries; I judged them according to
their conduct and their actions. ²⁰And wherever they went
among the nations they profaned my holy name, for it was
said of them, "These are the LORD's people, and yet they had
to leave his land." ²¹I had concern for my holy name, which
the house of Israel profaned among the nations where they
had gone.

²²Therefore say to the house of Israel, "This is what the
Sovereign LORD says: It is not for your sake, O house of
Israel, that I am going to do these things, but for the sake of
my holy name, which you have profaned among the nations
where you have gone. ²³I will show the holiness of my great
name, which has been profaned among the nations, the
name you have profaned among them. Then the nations will
know that I am the LORD, declares the Sovereign LORD, when
I show myself holy through you before their eyes.

²⁶"I will give you a new heart and put a new spirit in you; I
will remove from you your heart of stone and give you a
heart of flesh. ²⁷And I will put my Spirit in you and move
you to follow my decrees and be careful to keep my laws.
²⁸You will live in the land I gave your forefathers; you will be
my people, and I will be your God. ³¹Then you will
remember your evil ways and wicked deeds, and you will
loathe yourselves for your sins and detestable practices. ³²I
want you to know that I am not doing this for your sake,
declares the Sovereign LORD. Be ashamed and disgraced for
your conduct, O house of Israel!

³⁶"Then the nations around you that remain will know
that I the LORD have rebuilt what was destroyed and have
replanted what was desolate. I the LORD have spoken, and I
will do it."

³⁷This is what the Sovereign LORD says: Once again I will
yield to the plea of the house of Israel and do this for them: I
will make their people as numerous as sheep, ³⁸as numerous
as the flocks for offerings at Jerusalem during her appointed

feasts. So will the ruined cities be filled with flocks of people. Then they will know that I am the LORD.

Ezekiel 36:16–38, the context of these chosen verses, tells us that it was because of the LORD's concern for his name that he was bringing about the restoration (vv. 21–23). Under this purpose are subsumed the new covenant (vv. 26–27), the elements from Sinai (v. 27), and the Abrahamic promises (v. 28). The revelatory formula occurs in this context both with regard to Israel (v. 38) and the nations (vv. 23, 36).

Ezekiel 37:24–28

24My servant David will be king over them, and they will all have one shepherd. They will follow my laws and be careful to keep my decrees. 25They will live in the land I gave to my servant Jacob, the land where your fathers lived. They and their children and their children's children will live there forever, and David my servant will be their prince forever. 26I will make a covenant of peace with them; it will be an everlasting covenant. I will establish them and increase their numbers, and I will put my sanctuary among them forever. 27My dwelling place will be with them; I will be their God, and they will be my people. 28Then the nations will know that I the LORD make Israel holy, when my sanctuary is among them forever.

This brief passage referring specifically to David, the laws (Sinai), the land (the Patriarchs), and the new covenant, includes the election formula (v. 27) and ties it all together with the revelatory formula (v. 28).

Isaiah 43:25–28

25I, even I, am he who blots out
    your transgressions, for my own sake,
    and remembers your sins no more.
26Review the past for me,
    let us argue the matter together;
    state the case for your innocence.
27Your first father sinned;
    your spokesmen rebelled against me.
28So I will disgrace the dignitaries of your temple,

and I will consign Jacob to destruction
and Israel to scorn.

On rare occasions the Old Testament speaks specifically of blotting out sins. Even then the cited purpose is revelatory. This text speaks of the blotting out of sin not done principally for the sake of the sinner, but for the sake of the name of Yahweh. Revelation is identified as the objective even when redemptive or soteric elements are present.

Isaiah 48:9–11

9 For my own name's sake I delay my wrath;
   for the sake of my praise I hold it back from you,
   so as not to cut you off.
10 See, I have refined you, though not as silver;
   I have tested you in the furnace of affliction.
11 For my own sake, for my own sake, I do this.
   How can I let myself be defamed?
   I will not yield my glory to another.

Likewise God's delay of punishment is also said to have a revelatory purpose.

Jeremiah 14:21

21 For the sake of your name do not despise us;
   do not dishonor your glorious throne.
   Remember your covenant with us
   and do not break it.

When Yahweh is doing something for his own name's sake he is doing it as a matter of revelation concerning his nature.[22] Additionally, we must not lose sight of the ultimate goal of God's program, articulated here, that his glory be manifest. At times, as proven by verse twenty-one, we see this revelatory concern coupled explicitly with the covenant.

Isaiah 43:10–15

10 "You are my witnesses," declares the Lord,
   "and my servant whom I have chosen,
so that you may know and believe me
   and understand that I am he.

Before me no god was formed,
    nor will there be one after me.
11I, even I, am the LORD,
    and apart from me there is no savior.
12I have revealed and saved and proclaimed—
    I, and not some foreign god among you.
You are my witnesses," declares the LORD, "that I am God.
13Yes, and from ancient days I am he.
No one can deliver out of my hand.
When I act, who can reverse it?"
14This is what the LORD says—
    your Redeemer, the Holy One of Israel:
"For your sake I will send to Babylon
    and bring down as fugitives all the Babylonians,
    in the ships in which they took pride.
15I am the LORD, your Holy One,
    Israel's Creator, your King."

This passage not only gives a reason for election, but it summarizes the content of the revelation and indicates that God's intentions have been to reveal, save, and proclaim, and that Israel was chosen to serve as witness to what God had done: thus, its revelatory function. The last verse correlates to the three covenant phases: The LORD was revealed as Holy One in the giving of the law, he was Israel's Creator through the Abrahamic phase, and he is the King as revealed through the Davidic phase.

Passage Conclusions

The passages investigated above demonstrate that the entire series of covenants from Abraham through the new covenant are to be treated as achieving the particular purpose of revealing Yahweh to the nations as well as to Israel. Revealing "that I am Yahweh" is equivalent to revealing the nature of Yahweh.[23] These passages also clearly show that redemption, election, Torah, fulfilled promises, and possession of the land are each important motifs and each contributes to Yahweh's self-revelation—yet none of them is the objective of the covenant.

Furthermore, the interaction of these elements and the way in which they are woven together in the above contexts suggest that we are justified in some sense in speaking of *The Covenant*, which is made up of constituent phases of development. There will be opportunity to explore this in more depth as this theory unfolds in the following chapter. For the moment, suffice it to say that I believe there are elements of both continuity and discontinuity that must be recognized. As for the present model, I will recognize the continuity by speaking of The Covenant, and the discontinuity by speaking of the various phases in the development of the covenant.[24]

EXCURSUS: TRANSITION FROM GENESIS 1–11

In view of the interest in history evident in the Pentateuch and Former Prophets (Josh.–2 Kings), one might be inclined to think of Genesis 1–11 as an introduction to the history of Israel. In contrast, I would suggest that much of the Pentateuch and the Former Prophets comprise not a history of Israel, but a history of the covenant. It even would be difficult to comprehend the selection logic of the editor of the primeval history of Genesis 1–11 if that section were to be taken as an introduction of the story of Israel's election as the people of God. It makes much more sense that it be an introduction to God's program of revelation. How did it come about that people needed a revelation of Yahweh? Why did he not just keep in contact from the start? Genesis tells the story of how God created humankind in fellowship with him, but also relates how that relationship was destroyed by the Fall. The destruction of all but Noah and his family in the flood gave humanity a second opportunity to maintain a relationship, but again sin interfered.

The primeval history concludes with the important account of the Tower of Babel. Urbanization in Mesopotamia had provided fertile ground for the development of a new paganism aptly represented in the symbolism of the ziggurat. The Tower of Babel represented the definitive formulation of a brand of paganism that pervaded the ancient Near East in which mythologized deity was portrayed as having all the foibles of humanity. In so doing, humanity remade deity in its own image.[25] The perception of God that swept the ancient world was incapable of providing a sound basis for a relationship with the one true God. The result was the need for God to vouchsafe an accurate revelation of himself. He therefore instituted a revelatory program by means of the covenant. In this way chapters 1–11 of Genesis show why there was a need for a revelatory program and lead into the details of how God embarked on that program using the mechanism of the covenant.

NOTES

[1]O. Palmer Robertson, *The Christ of the Covenants* (Phillipsburg, N.J.: Presbyterian and Reformed, 1980), 293–94.

[2]N. Stonehouse, "Special Revelation as Scriptural" in *Revelation and the Bible* ed. Carl F. H. Henry (Grand Rapids: Baker, 1958), 77. See also G. Vos, *Biblical Theology* (Grand Rapids: Eerdmans, 1948), 89–90.

[3]Robert L. Saucy, *The Case for Progressive Dispensationalism* (Grand Rapids: Zondervan, 1993), 40. His discussion of Israel's revelatory role (311–19) is remarkably close to the position I take.

[4]W. W. Klein, *The New Chosen People: A Corporate View of Election* (Grand Rapids: Zondervan, 1990), 43 (see also p. 32).

[5]W. Eichrodt, *Theology of the Old Testament* (Philadelphia: Westminster, 1961), I:14.

[6]Ibid.

[7]Ibid., I:55–56. The letters *D* and *P* refer to the Graf-Wellhausen Documentary Hypothesis, which is outlined in Andrew E. Hill and John H. Walton, *A Survey of the Old Testament* (Grand Rapids: Zondervan, 1991), 78.

[8]Ibid., I:58.

[9]G. E. Wright, *God Who Acts* (London: SCM, 1952), 57.

[10]J. Jocz, *The Covenant* (Grand Rapids: Eerdmans, 1968).

[11]Ibid., 256.

[12]Ibid., 270.

[13]Seock-Tae Sohn, *The Divine Election of Israel* (Grand Rapids: Eerdmans, 1991), 196–97.

[14]G. Hasel, *Old Testament Theology: Basic Issues in the Current Debate* (Grand Rapids: Eerdmans, 1972), 100.

[15]R. E. Clements, *Old Testament Theology: A Fresh Approach* (Atlanta: John Knox, 1978), 103.

[16]Robert Saucy, "Israel and the Church: A Case for Discontinuity," in *Continuity and Discontinuity*, ed. John S. Feinberg (Wheaton: Crossway, 1988), 256.

[17]John S. Feinberg, "Systems of Discontinuity" in *Continuity and Discontinuity*, 85. For an excellent comparison of dispensationalism and nondispensationalism, see Saucy, *The Case for Progressive Dispensationalism*, 21–29.

[18]D. Hillers, *Covenant: The History of a Biblical Idea* (Baltimore: Johns Hopkins, 1969), 122. See also H. Huffmon, "The Treaty Background of Hebrew YADA," *BASOR* 181 (1966): 31–37; and H. Huffmon and S. Parker, "A Further Note on the Treaty Background of Hebrew YADA," *BASOR* 184 (1966): 36–38.

[19]I see no substantial difference between "know" and "acknowledge" in these contexts. "Acknowledge" involves at least a *mental response*. It may or may not involve a change in conduct or worldview and therefore is not an intrinsically relational concept.

[20]Following the analysis of R. Garr, "The Grammar and Interpretation of Exodus 6:3" *JBL* 111 (1992): 407.

[21]Ibid., 406.

[22]J. A. Motyer, *The Revelation of the Divine Name* (London: Tyndale, 1959), 13–24.

[23]Ibid., 397. See also the discussion of R. Rendtorff, "The Concept of Revelation in Ancient Israel," in *Revelation as History*, ed. W. Pannenberg (New York: Macmillan, 1968), 25–53, esp. 41–44.

[24]I understand that this will require a fuller investigation of passages such as 2 Corinthians 3 and Hebrews 8 that delineate old/new and first/second distinctions, but these will be addressed in their proper place.

[25]For a full discussion of the Tower of Babel, see John H. Walton, "The Mesopotamian Background of the Tower of Babel and Its Implications," *BBR* (forthcoming).

3

THE NUMBER OF COVENANTS

There are many covenants in the Bible. We have already discussed the fact that the Hebrew word for covenant may refer to agreements on many different levels within society. When we restrict the category of covenants to those between God and man, however, we are dealing with a much smaller number. If we depend on the biblical text to identify such covenants for us, we find the first covenant in the time of Noah.

While it is typical for the various systems of theology to include all of the covenants and to weave them all into their systems, the proposal under consideration in this book does not lend itself to such systematization. As will be demonstrated later, the constituent phases of what I am calling The Covenant each contain an element of election. It is this characteristic feature that binds them together. Additionally, in The Covenant each new phase consistently establishes points of contact with the previous phases. The covenant with Noah, however, stands outside and separate on both these counts. Therefore, while the covenant with Noah clearly represents an agreement between God and man, the absence of the characteristic elements that define the other covenants in the text suggest it is entirely distinct from The Covenant and not to be included in God's program of special revelation.[1]

DIFFERING VIEWS ABOUT THE COVENANTS

Seven Covenants

In classic dispensationalism one can encounter from four to as many as eight dispensations, each governed by a covenant. The standard works, however, generally identify seven dispensations. Within dispensationalism, the category of covenant is subordinated to the category of dispensation and the focus of study is on the dispensation rather than on the covenant itself.[2] By relating each of the covenants to different dispensations there is a higher level of discontinuity established between the covenants. Rather than addressing the goal, objective, or purpose of the covenant(s), study of the dispensations is often more concerned with God's governance of human affairs.

Two Covenants

Classic covenant theology has historically viewed history as divided into two covenants, the covenant of works and the covenant of grace. The covenant of works was the norm prior to the Fall of Adam at which time the covenant of grace replaced it, in essence providing a means of redemption. Though the covenant of works is not mentioned explicitly in Scripture it is inferred from the statements and situation in Genesis 2 and 3.

One Covenant

In reality, the covenants that are mentioned in the pages of Scripture and that span the history of fallen humanity are seen by covenant theologians as being a unified group, as expressed by O. Palmer Robertson.

> The cumulative evidence of the Scriptures points definitely toward the unified character of the biblical covenants. God's multiple bonds with his people ultimately unite into a single relationship. Particular details of the covenants may vary. A definite line of progress may be noted. Yet the covenants of God are one.[3]

In this view the unity is based on the redemptive (i.e., redemptive + soteric) element that is interpreted as the purpose of the covenant and includes the covenant with Noah.

Promissory and Administrative Covenants

In recent approaches that seek to take a biblical-theology approach it is common to see a few different categories of covenant. Thomas McComiskey differentiates between promissory covenants (e.g., Abraham and David) and administrative covenants (e.g., Moses and the new covenant).

CONTINUITY AND DISCONTINUITY

Everyone agrees that God made covenants with Abraham, Moses, David, etc. How the various covenants are related to one another and how they are fitted into a larger pattern are where the differences arise. All of the positions identified above see some continuity and some discontinuity between the covenants. They merely vary on how much of each they see.

As in the discussion of the purpose of the covenant, there is much in all of the positions that is entirely agreeable to the hypothesis we are considering. It is not the intention of this book to criticize other positions (nor to critique them in detail), but to try to integrate all the best aspects into one central hypothesis. The question, then, is not whether there is continuity or discontinuity, for both exist, but how each should be viewed in relation to the covenant phases.

In the hypothesis presented here, continuity exists as a result of the opinion that each of the covenants, Abraham through the new covenant, plays an integral part in God's program of revelation. Each is a part of a single, unified program of revelation. The enactment or primacy of one does not mean the nullification or subordination of another. None of these covenants replaces the one before it—each supplements what has come before.

In the same manner, if each covenant supplements the previous covenant(s), then each has a unique contribution to make: thus, the discontinuity. Rather than see each covenant as a separate entity, they are here considered to be phases of development; subagreements to the main agreement. Again, this is not an entirely new concept, as can be seen from Robertson's work, among others.

> At those points in history in which God initiated the new covenantal relationships under Moses and David, evidence indicates that God was intending to bring to a further stage of development the same redemption that had been promised earlier.[4]

It must be noted, however, that the discontinuity that exists between the new covenant and the previous phases is much more marked. The election of Israel as the people of God in the book of Exodus did not in any way mitigate the election of the family of Abraham. Neither did the election of the Davidic dynasty have any effect on the elect status of Abraham's family or the people of Israel. But, as I will suggest and defend in chapters 7 and 8, the election of all believers as people of God in the new covenant *did* bring an end to the elect status of ethnic Israel. Though the new covenant is organically related to the previous phases, I would see a greater degree of discontinuity between the new covenant and those previous phases. This justifies the New Testament use of terminology such as "first" covenant (Heb. 8:13) and "old" covenant (2 Cor. 3:14).[5]

In this model of The Covenant, then, I will speak of two covenants[6] organically related to one another (one "rolls over" into the other, much like investments might be rolled over). The new covenant is founded on the completion or the fulfillment of the old covenant and thus provides an organic relationship.[7] Because of this organic relationship, the two together comprise The Covenant.

The discontinuity among the covenant phases is expressed in that each has its own distinct elements of revelation and election. Their continuity is expressed in that each features the categories of revelation and election, as well as a link to the Abrahamic promises, connections to transitional periods of history, and ultimate integration into the person and role of Christ. Each of these elements will be discussed briefly below, followed by a fuller summary of the progressive development of the covenant phases.

Phases Linked to One Another

As we found in the analysis of passages in chapter 2, there are numerous verses that link the covenants to one another.

- The covenant at Sinai is linked to the Abrahamic promises (Ex. 6:2–8; Deut. 7:7–9)
- The covenant with David is linked to Sinai (2 Sam. 7:22–24)
- The new covenant is linked to Sinai (Jer. 31:33; Ezek. 36:26–28)
- The new covenant is linked to David (Ezek. 34:23–27)
- The new covenant is linked to Abraham (Ezek. 36:24–28)
- All four are linked together in Ezekiel 37:24–28

Phases Linked to Transitional Periods of History

The first major transition for the people of the covenant is comprised of the four hundred plus years in Egypt spent growing from a small family to a verifiable people group. This transitional period ends when they are brought out of Egypt and a new phase of the covenant is established at Sinai.

Another easily identifiable transition begins with the fall of the house of David and of Jerusalem as well as the destruction of the Temple in 587 B.C. The resultant Exile is only the beginning of this transition, which is brought to an end by Christ's inauguration of the new covenant phase.

A third, and much less recognized, transition takes place at the end of the Judges period. In this transition, Israel is not absent from the land; the ark of the covenant is—an act of self-imposed exile that the LORD initiates (1 Sam. 4–6).[8] Immediately upon the reinstallation of the ark (2 Sam. 6) in Jerusalem (putting an end to this transition period) the Davidic phase of the covenant is put into place (2 Sam. 7).

Phases Characterized by a New Aspect of Revelation

Except for the first transitional period (the sojourn in Egypt), these periods are the result of God's judgment on Israel for their failure to respond to the revelation of the previous phase. Despite these failures, however, God sovereignly carries forward his program of revelation because God's revelatory objectives can be achieved with or without Israel's help. If they cooperate, there is benefit for them. If they fail there is punishment. God's program is never in jeopardy, but Israel's enjoyment of covenant benefits is always subject to review. So it is that the phases of the covenant with their respective revelatory foci march inexorably on. The link of revelation joins the phases of the covenant together into a unified purpose, respectively demonstrating God's faithfulness, holiness, sovereignty (kingship), and soteric plan.

Phases Characterized by a New Aspect of Election

Though election is one of the predominant themes of the Old Testament, it is subordinate to the covenant and a component part of it. "Election is motivated by the covenant rather than the covenant being motivated by election."[9] God chooses (1) Abraham in order to make a covenant with him, (2) Israel to be his people, (3) the Davidic dynasty to provide the only divinely sanctioned kingship, and (4) believers to be the heirs of salvation. These are the primary elective acts of God in the Bible and each is connected to a primary phase of the development of the covenant. The theme of election can therefore be seen as unifying those phases of development.

Phases Brought Together in the Person and Role of Christ

The major titles that are attached confessionally to Jesus are Son of God, Messiah, and Savior. These can be seen to relate to the three phases of covenant development. The holy character of God (revealed at Sinai), the kingship of God (revealed in David), and the soteric plan of God (revealed in the new covenant) are all drawn together in Christ and fulfilled in him.

THE FRAMEWORK OF GOD'S PLAN OF REVELATION

Throughout the ages the book of Esther has always been an enigma and sometimes has been an embarrassment to those who have studied the Old Testament. Foremost among the features considered to be embarrassing is the inexplicable failure to mention even once the name of God. Certainly anyone who believes in God cannot help but see that God is behind the events of the book, but at times the author appears to go out of his way to avoid any reference to deity. The hypothesis under investigation in this book offers some insight into this issue. We will not dwell long on it, but will use it as an introduction to the idea of the covenant phases constituting a program of revelation.

The book of Esther makes the most sophisticated and extensive use of irony in biblical narrative.[10] Irony is defined as "the incongruity between the actual result of a sequence of events and the expected result." In Esther, this incongruity recurs again and again because of hidden information. The whole plot of the Esther narrative is built on hidden information, and the fact that the readers are privy to some of the hidden information helps them to appreciate the unfolding drama. The most poignant example of irony may be when Haman goes to the court planning to ask for the execution of Mordecai and is called in by the king to give advice on how to reward an unnamed official whom the reader knows to be Mordecai but whom Haman infers to be himself. Though dozens of examples can be drawn from this short book, this is irony at its best. Irony operates when there is more going on than meets the eye. It is this literary device that helps the author of Esther bring out a theological truth. With God, too, there is always more going on than meets the eye, and indeed, more that he is doing than anyone can imagine or anticipate.

The key thing that must be noticed about deliverance in the book of Esther is that God acts surreptitiously. His "involvement" is one of the main pieces of hidden information. The very centrality of the *pur* and the resulting celebration of Purim emphasize this fact. Every Israelite knew that fate, or the lots, are in the hand of God. But to Haman (who used them) they were depersonalized—not connected to God. All of this indicates what is obvious in the book: There are two distinct ways to view the turn of events there recorded. The events are either a curious sequence of circumstance or are covert sovereignty. The absence of reference to God, I believe, intentionally leaves this question hanging in the balance.[11]

If God is acting surreptitiously, through means that could easily be considered mere circumstance, then we must conclude that he does not intend his act of deliverance to serve as revelation to all those who witness it, for his role (even in the text) is concealed rather than revealed. This is a far cry from how God had previously conducted his deliverances. The Exodus was accompanied by mighty acts of miraculous power that all could see. God's revelatory intentions are effective as Rahab confesses for all the Canaanites:

> [10]We have heard how the LORD dried up the water of the Red
> Sea for you when you came out of Egypt, and what you did
> to Sihon and Og, the two kings of the Amorites east of the
> Jordan, whom you completely destroyed. [11]When we heard
> of it our hearts melted and everyone's courage failed because
> of you, for the LORD your God is God in heaven above and on
> the earth below. (Josh. 2:10–11)

Here God's intervention in history served a very clear revelatory function. Similarly, in that other great deliverance, the return from the Exile, the prophetic word was used to offer clear revelation concerning its supernatural perpetrator. God's deliverance was intended to be a light to the nations that all would see and to which all would respond. What is startling about the book of Esther, then, is that God does not precede his deliverance with great prophetic pronouncements, neither does he perform the deliverance by miraculous signs and wonders; instead he stays behind the curtain, apparently content to let onlookers conclude what they will about how this deliverance occurred. This policy, I suggest, is an indication of an important theological shift that takes place in the postexilic period. To understand it we must revert to some basic theological issues.

When God initiated the covenant by making promises to Abraham, he indicated both the benefits Abraham and his descendants would reap as well as what function they would serve in his plan. Not only would Abraham's family be given a land, and not only would they become a great nation,[12] but all the nations of the earth would be blessed through them.[13] How was this blessing to come about? What is the nature of it? The Old Testament never explicitly defines what is entailed in this blessing, but it does make reference to the blessing on a number of occasions and these comprise our point of departure.

Some blessings on those outside of Israel are identified even in the chapters of Genesis. Individuals such as Lot, Abimelek, and Laban all benefited directly from contact with Abraham, Isaac, and Jacob.

> The Yahwist expounds his kerygma through the patriarchal narrative. He deals with "all the families of the earth" using as examples the Moabites, Ammonites, Philistines, and Arameans. How are they to find blessing in Israel? By Israel's intercession with Yahweh on the example of Abraham; by readiness for peaceful agreement on the pattern of Isaac; by economic aid on the model of Jacob. Yahweh created the prerequisite by fulfilling the promise of increase and expansion. In what way is blessing found through all of this? Blessing is found in annulment of guilt or punishment, in community life without strife, in effective material aid.[14]

Likewise the prophets indicate a particular blessing that may accrue to the nations through Israel. A prime example is found in Jeremiah 4:1-2.

> [1]"If you will return, O Israel,
> return to me," declares the LORD.
> "If you put your detestable idols out of my sight
> and no longer go astray,
> [2]and if in a truthful, just and righteous way
> you swear, 'As surely as the LORD lives,'
> then the nations will be blessed by him
> and in him they will glory."

In this context the nations stand to benefit in some way from Israel's repentance. Robert Carroll understands the gain to the nations in terms of an opportunity for a relationship with Yahweh.

Now if the nation can sort out its cultic matters, discover exclusive devotion to Yahweh, then the nations round about will benefit greatly from such a turning. . . . Israel's turning means the transformation of the nations.[15]

Further interpretation of the blessing on the nations comes from the writers of the New Testament. Both Peter and Paul connect the blessing specifically to the salvation that is available to the Gentiles through Christ.

Acts 3:24–26

[24]Indeed, all the prophets from Samuel on, as many as have spoken, have foretold these days. [24]And you are heirs of the prophets and of the covenant God made with your fathers. He said to Abraham, "Through your offspring all peoples on earth will be blessed." [26]When God raised up his servant, he sent him first to you to bless you by turning each of you from your wicked ways.

Galatians 3:6–14

[6]Consider Abraham: "He believed God, and it was credited to him as righteousness." [7]Understand, then, that those who believe are children of Abraham. [8]The Scripture foresaw that God would justify the Gentiles by faith, and announced the gospel in advance to Abraham: "All nations will be blessed through you." [9]So those who have faith are blessed along with Abraham, the man of faith.

[10]All who rely on observing the law are under a curse, for it is written: "Cursed is everyone who does not continue to do everything written in the Book of the Law." [11]Clearly no one is justified before God by the law, because, "The righteous will live by faith." [12]The law is not based on faith; on the contrary, "The man who does these things will live by them." [13]Christ redeemed us from the curse of the law by becoming a curse for us, for it is written: "Cursed is everyone who is hung on a tree." [14]He redeemed us in order that the blessing given to Abraham might come to the Gentiles through Christ Jesus, so that by faith we might receive the promise of the Spirit.

Some interpreters use these passages as evidence that the blessing of Abraham, which God extended to the nations, meant always and only the blessing of salvation to come.

> A blessing so great that its effect shall extend to "all the families of the earth" can be thought of only in connection with the promised Savior. This word, therefore, is definitely messianic and determines that the Messiah is to emerge from the line of Abram.[16]

Given the variations that occur within the pages of Scripture, it is our task not to choose one variation over another, but to find the common ground that binds them together. Before proceeding with that, however, to these passages that make explicit reference to the blessings on the nations we must add a number of passages that refer to a benefit gained by the nations through Israel, though not specifically identified in the text as a blessing.

Joshua 4:21-24

21He said to the Israelites, "In the future when your descendants ask their fathers, 'What do these stones mean?' 22tell them, 'Israel crossed the Jordan on dry ground.' 23For the LORD your God dried up the Jordan before you until you had crossed over. The LORD your God did to the Jordan just what he had done to the Red Sea when he dried it up before us until we had crossed over. 24He did this so that all the peoples of the earth might know that the hand of the LORD is powerful and so that you might always fear the LORD your God."

Here the act of God referred to is not specifically an act of deliverance, but a miraculous indicator of divine support. The expected result for all the peoples of the earth is that they might have evidence that affirmed God's power.

Isaiah 49:25-26

25But this is what the LORD says:

"Yes, captives will be taken from warriors,
    and plunder retrieved from the fierce;

> I will contend with those who contend with you,
>   and your children I will save.
> 26I will make your oppressors eat their own flesh;
>   they will be drunk on their own blood,
>   as with wine.
> Then all mankind will know
>   that I, the Lord, am your Savior,
>   your Redeemer, the Mighty One of Jacob."

At first reading this passage seems hardly to represent a benefit or gain for the nations. Upon closer examination, however, it is important to differentiate between the oppressors, who are being punished, and all mankind, who will benefit from the lesson. This passage is significant for two reasons. First, it should be noticed that at the end of verse twenty-five there stands an unmistakable reference to Genesis 12:3. "I will contend with those who contend with you" is strikingly reminiscent of "Whoever curses you I will curse." It is therefore not overly imaginative to relate the resulting "then all mankind will know . . ." to the next clause in the Abrahamic blessing, "all peoples on earth will be blessed through you." A second item of significance is that in this context the specific content of the revelation is of God as deliverer (redeemer), but in a very specific militaristic sense.

Ezekiel 36:21–23

21I had concern for my holy name, which the house of Israel profaned among the nations where they had gone.

22Therefore say to the house of Israel, "This is what the Sovereign Lord says: It is not for your sake, O house of Israel, that I am going to do these things, but for the sake of my holy name, which you have profaned among the nations where you have gone. 23I will show the holiness of my great name, which has been profaned among the nations, the name you have profaned among them. Then the nations will know that I am the Lord, declares the Sovereign Lord, when I show myself holy through you before their eyes."

The last sentence is the most significant one here. God's holiness being revealed to and acknowledged by the nations is being accomplished through Israel (the same preposition is found in Genesis 12:3). The blessing procured by the nations through Israel is the knowledge of God and it is made available, as the text states, for the sake of God's holy name.

Ezekiel 37:24–28

24My servant David will be king over them, and they will all have one shepherd. They will follow my laws and be careful to keep my decrees. 25They will live in the land I gave to my servant Jacob, the land where your fathers lived. They and their children and their children's children will live there forever, and David my servant will be their prince forever. 26I will make a covenant of peace with them; it will be an everlasting covenant. I will establish them and increase their numbers, and I will put my sanctuary among them forever. 27My dwelling place will be with them; I will be their God, and they will be my people. 28Then the nations will know that I the LORD make Israel holy, when my sanctuary is among them forever.

In Ezekiel 36 it had been God's treatment of Israel that served as blessing (by means of revelation) to the nations. Unfortunately there is not a direct connection to the covenant in that passage. Ezekiel 37, however, clarifies that connection. Here we find all of the major elements of the covenant connected to the same purpose.

Ezekiel 39:21–24

21I will display my glory among the nations, and all the nations will see the punishment I inflict and the hand I lay upon them. 22From that day forward the house of Israel will know that I am the LORD their God. 23And the nations will know that the people of Israel went into exile for their sin, because they were unfaithful to me. So I hid my face from them and handed them over to their enemies, and they all fell by the sword. 24I dealt with them according to their uncleanness and their offenses, and I hid my face from them.

GOD'S PLAN

GOAL: RELATIONSHIP
OBJECTIVE: REVELATION
MECHANISM: COVENANT
INSTRUMENT: ISRAEL

Finally, we see, in this passage, that the revelation that serves as a lesson to the nations comes from the fact that God has punished his people Israel.

Now, based on the range of benefits identified as blessings on non-Israelites and related to the promise made to Abraham, and based on the benefits that accrue to the nations through the Israelites, it is possible to propose an interpretation of Genesis 12:3 that takes all of this information into consideration.

I propose that the nature of the blessing on the nations is that, through Abraham's family, God revealed himself.[17] The law was given through them, the Scripture was written by them, and their history became the public record of God's attributes in action. Then to climax it all, his own Son came through them and provided salvation for the world. Israel was the chosen people of God, not in the sense that they always obeyed or believed; not in the sense that they were all automatically heirs to salvation; but in the sense that they were the instrument, and sometimes the medium, of his own self-revelation. It is expected and proper that the New Testament should emphasize the blessing of salvation through Christ, for that is the ultimate provision of the way that relationship could be achieved. It is the climax and culmination of God's program of revelation.

In summary of the conclusions of this chapter I would propose that there is *one* covenant in two major stages, Old and New. The former is articulated in phases that are linked, yet distinct. The purpose of this one covenant is to serve as a mechanism for God's self-revelation. That purpose is expressed in the original proclamation of the covenant in terms of Abraham and his family serving as instruments of God's blessing on the world. That blessing was identified as God's revelation of himself and his plan, especially (eventually) his plan of salvation which made relationship with him possible.

NOTES

[1]Some argue that Noah's covenant provides a context for the others; e.g., R. T. Beckwith, "The Unity and Diversity of God's Covenants" *TB* 38 (1987): 107; it is unrelated in the sense that it could arguably be seen as establishing God's program of *general* revelation, but lacks any element of special revelation.

[2]"Dispensation" here refers to a particular period of time in God's plan characterized by features distinguishing it from other periods, e.g., "dispensation of law." "Covenant" refers to the agreement which governs and defines that dispensation. Covenants may be identified as "biblical" covenants, articulated as a covenant in the Bible, or "theological" covenants constructed by theologians, often composites of several biblical covenants.

[3]O. Palmer Robertson, *The Christ of the Covenants* (Phillipsburg, N.J.: Presbyterian and Reformed, 1980), 28.

[4]Ibid., 29. See also F. C. Fensham, "Covenant, Promise and Expectation in the Bible" *Theologische Zeitschrift* 23 (1967): 305–22.

[5]David Dorsey, "The Law of Moses and the Christian: A Compromise" *JETS* 34 (1991): 325.

[6]Much in agreement with Kenneth Barker, "The Scope and Center of Old and New Testament Theology and Hope" in *Dispensationalism, Israel and the Church*, ed. C. A. Blaising and D. L. Bock (Grand Rapids: Zondervan, 1992), 295.

[7]This view of the new covenant is not unlike that proposed by W. Kaiser, *Toward an Old Testament Theology* (Grand Rapids: Zondervan, 1978): 232–34, though it is developed differently. See also his article "The Old Promise and the New Covenant: Jer. 31:31–34" *JETS* 15 (1972): 11–23. I would not choose "renewed" as the appropriate description, but have no major objections to it.

[8]This view is well articulated by Anthony Campbell, *The Ark Narrative* (Missoula: Scholars Press, 1975).

[9]Seock-Tae Sohn, *The Divine Election of Israel* (Grand Rapids: Eerdmans, 1991), 194.

[10]More specifically referred to as "reversal" or "peripety"; See Michael V. Fox, *Character and Ideology in the Book of Esther* (Columbia: University of South Carolina Press, 1991), 158–63.

[11]See also *NIV Study Bible*, 719.

[12]I would agree with those who see these promises as reflecting the blessing of Genesis 1:28, though I do not agree that such an association identifies the promises as soteriological. See J. Sailhamer, *The Pentateuch as*

Narrative (Grand Rapids: Zondervan, 1992), 139; N. T. Wright, *The Climax of the Covenant* (Minneapolis: Fortress, 1991), 21–23.

[13]I am not at all convinced that this should be translated as a result clause (as per W. VanGemeren, *The Progress of Redemption* [Grand Rapids: Zondervan, 1988], 107; and W. C. Kaiser, *Toward an Old Testament Theology* [Grand Rapids: Zondervan, 1978], 87). The grammatical construction is a waw-consecutive imperfect, which is not one of the several ways that Hebrew conveys result unless it is preceded by a volitional form (e.g., cohortative, cf. Waltke and O'Connor, *Biblical Hebrew Syntax* [Winona Lake: Eisenbrauns, 1990], 39.2.2).

[14]W. Brueggemann and H. W. Wolff, *The Vitality of Old Testament Traditions* (Atlanta: John Knox, 1975), 59.

[15]Robert P. Carroll, *Jeremiah* (Philadelphia: Westminster, 1986), 156.

[16]H. C. Leupold, *Exposition of Genesis* (Grand Rapids: Baker, 1942), I:413.

[17]Galatians 3 relates the blessing specifically to the salvation that comes through faith, but does not limit the blessing to that. The Gentiles benefited from the entire revelation process that culminated in the provision of a means of salvation available to all through faith as Paul is stressing in Galatians 3.

4

THE PHASES OF THE COVENANT

THE INITIATORY PHASE OF THE COVENANT

In Genesis 12 God called Abram from his land with the prospect of providing certain benefits. When Abram accepted the offer the agreement was ratified into a covenant in Genesis 15. This was the initiatory phase of the covenant. In it God chooses Abram as the one to whom the offer is made and with whom the covenant relationship is formed (Gen. 18:19). God begins the revelation of himself in this initiatory phase as one who is faithful to keep his promises. This pattern—featuring an element of election and a main focus of revelation—is maintained throughout each of the successive phases of development.

From Ratification to Phase One

The Patriarchal period ends with Jacob's family all going down to Egypt. The first transitional period, as previously mentioned, is the sojourn in Egypt. Although the promises have been made and the covenant ratified, the Israelites possess no land, they are not a great nation, and they are not a blessing. The Exodus marks the end of the transitional period and it is at this juncture that the first phase of covenantal development occurs. At Sinai the development of the covenant features a new point of election. Previously God had chosen Abraham and had promised, "I will establish my covenant as

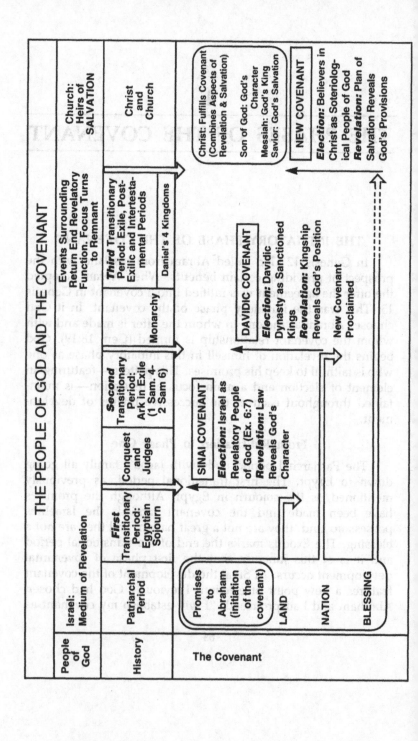

THE PEOPLE OF GOD AND THE COVENANT

People of God	Israel: Medium of Revelation						Church: Heirs of SALVATION
History	Patriarchal Period	*First* Transitionary Period: Egyptian Sojourn	Conquest and Judges	*Second* Transitionary Period: Ark in Exile (1 Sam. 4- 2 Sam 6)	Monarchy	*Third* Transitionary Period: Exile, Post-Exilic and Intertesta-mental Periods	Christ and Church

Events Surrounding Return End Revelatory Function. Focus Turns to Remnant

Daniel's 4 Kingdoms

Christ: Fulfills Covenant (Combines Aspects of Revelation & Salvation)

Son of God: God's Character
Messiah: God's King
Savior: God's Salvation

NEW COVENANT

Election: Believers in Christ as Soteriological People of God
Revelation: Plan of Salvation Reveals God's Provisions

DAVIDIC COVENANT

Election: Davidic Dynasty as Sanctioned Kings
Revelation: Kingship Reveals God's Position

New Covenant Proclaimed

SINAI COVENANT

Election: Israel as Revelatory People of God (Ex. 6:7)
Revelation: Law Reveals God's Character

Promises to Abraham (initiation of the covenant)

LAND

NATION

BLESSING

The Covenant

an everlasting covenant between me and you and your descendants after you for the generations to come, to be your God and the God of your descendants after you" (Gen. 17:7). But now God expands his election to Israel: "I will take you *as my own people*, and I will be your God. Then you will know that I am the LORD your God, who brought you out from under the yoke of the Egyptians" (Ex. 6:7, italics mine). They are now God's chosen people, chosen to reveal him to the rest of the world, as the context indicates. They have become the "revelatory" people of God.

Likewise the development of the covenant at Sinai featured a new point of revelation in the Law that had been given to Moses. Of course it was not the legislation that was necessarily new, but the revelation of the character of God as the basis for that legislation: "Be holy because I, the LORD your God, am holy" (Lev. 19:2). The most significant function of the law is not as a judicial tool for society (as such, it is in many ways obsolete), but as a revelation of the character of God (cf., 1 Peter 1:13–15; for a more detailed treatment of this topic see chapter 10). This phase of covenant development also emphasizes the fulfillment of the promise of the land as God brings Israel to Canaan and oversees their possession of it.[1]

From Phase One to Phase Two

During the period of the Judges, the Israelites, a people living in the land, are in many ways still not considered a nation, as the book is at pains to tell us ("in those days there was no king in Israel"). It is a period of failure because the revelation that God gave at Sinai fails to have the desired effect. The unfaithfulness of the people was bad enough, but when the priesthood also degenerated (cf. Judges 17–21 and Eli's sons), God took action by undertaking a self-imposed exile, signaled by the capture of the ark.[2] This second transitional period is not as widely recognized as the others, but it is clearly indicated in the text. The theology is articulated in Psalm 78:56–72. Furthermore, the victory of the ark over the idol of Dagon demonstrates that the ark had left Israel by God's own choice; he had abandoned them. The transitional period is comprised

of Samuel's ministry and Saul's reign. The biblical text marks
the end of this transitional period with David's restoration of
the ark to centrality in Jerusalem, as recorded in 2 Samuel 6. It
should not be overlooked that the restoration is immediately
followed by the next phase of the development of the covenant—the Davidic covenant—recorded in 2 Samuel 7.[3]

The element of election that is featured in this new phase
of covenant development is, of course, the Davidic dynasty.
David and his descendants were chosen as sanctioned kings.
The new step of revelation emphasizes God's position as king,
theoretically to be reflected in the conduct and administration
of his human vice-regent and representative. This element,
though not stated explicitly in the presentation of the covenant
in 2 Samuel 7, can be demonstrated through a number of
different approaches to the textual material, including: (1) the
contrast between Saul and David, (2) the emphasis on Yahweh's kingship in the books of Samuel, (3) the role of the king,
(4) the royal psalms, and (5) lexical analysis.

Contrast Between Saul and David

Even in the opening narratives concerning Israelite kingship it is clear that human kingship can be a threat to divine
kingship. Saul is God's choice for king in fulfillment of the
people's distorted view of kingship. They are discontent having
"Yahweh of armies" lead them in battle; they want a king to
lead them out into battle. This desire for human leadership
constitutes a rejection of Yahweh's kingship.

> In 1 Samuel 8:7 Israel's request is interpreted as a rejection of
> Yahweh. The assumption behind this is that either Yahweh
> is and remains king, or a man steps into his place. This
> cannot be a rejection of all leaders so one must ask in what
> way kingship could mean a rejection of Yahweh. . . . It is
> Yahweh who saves and delivers Israel, and human kingship
> displaces Yahweh when Yahweh is no longer seen as being
> responsible for Israel's defense. That this is what Israel was
> doing in their request is confirmed by 1 Samuel 8:20. Israel
> has asked for a king who will "go out before us and fight our

battles." But this is the very language used of Yahweh in his role as the defender of Israel.[4]

In contrast to the people's distorted view, human kingship was supposed to serve as a reflection of what God's kingship was like. This required that the king see himself as a vassal of Yahweh.

> Ideologically, monarchy in Israel was acceptable only insofar as it was *not* "like [that of] all the other nations," that is, only insofar as the king was willing to acknowledge his subordination to the Great King and his designated spokesman.[5]

The representative and subordinate element is well-stated by Matitiahu Tsevat:

> The meaning of the kingship of God, according to the Bible, is the denial to man of the concentration and permanence of power. Power in society is God's. He is the only source of might, authority, command, and ownership of the land; He is the author of morals, law, and judgment; He guarantees freedom and a measure of equality; He is the leader of journeys in the desert and campaigns in the sown.[6]

The failure of Saul to provide the leadership expected by the people is evident in 1 Samuel 17. The battle with Goliath waits while Saul stays in his tent. David, meanwhile, sees perfectly well that it is not the combatants who win the battle, but God. Consequently he is not afraid to fight Goliath. Thus, David stands as "a man after God's own heart"—that is, a man of God's own choosing in accordance with his own criteria. This is an indication that the human king is understood to be a vassal to the divine king.[7] Aubrey R. Johnson goes so far as to consider the Spirit-endowed king "a potent extension of the divine Personality."[8]

The Emphasis of the Books of Samuel

The emphasis on God's kingship in the books of Samuel also demonstrates that the revelation of divine kingship is foremost in the mind of the author. This emphasis is evidenced by the frequent use of the title "Yahweh of armies" (*ṣeba'ot*) as

well as by the poetic inclusio of the books of Samuel in
Hannah's song (1 Sam. 2:1–10) and the last words of David
(2 Sam. 23:1–7).[9] In both of these poetic pieces, divine kingship
plays a significant role. Just as the Sinai covenant emphasized
the land, the Davidic covenant emphasizes the nation. In the
promises to the Patriarchs, the end result of having many
descendants was that they would become a great nation and
that kings would come from them (Gen. 17:1–6; 35:10–12). It is
the Davidic covenant that signals that this promise has become
reality.

The Role of the King

While it is certainly true that the king was entrusted with
modeling the keeping of the law and was judged on the basis of
how well he kept the law, these cannot be viewed as the only
criteria for evaluating his success. For example, Saul is clearly a
failure as king, and was treated as such, though the text never
suggests that he was not a keeper of the law. There is no
mention of the high places or apostate worship during his rule
and there is no formulary indictment concerning his not
keeping the law of Moses. How, then, was Saul's failure
articulated? The answer must be sought through an investigation of the role of the king in Israel. Gerald Gerbrandt has
persuasively argued that the king was viewed as the mediator
of the covenant.

> Since Israel's continued existence as a people on the land was
> dependent on her obedience to the covenant, and since the
> king's ultimate responsibility was to insure this continued
> existence, the king's role was then to make sure that the
> covenant was observed in Israel. Practically, he could be
> called the *covenant administrator*.[10]

The role of covenant administrator had several aspects to it
and was laid out in a charter of kingship that constituted the
agreement that was formalized between God, king, and people
(1 Sam. 10:25; 11:14; 13:13–14; 15:24; additionally, see 2 Sam.
5:3; 2 Kings 11:12; 23:3). The elements included in this charter
suggest that the king's responsibility in this role was to make

sure that the Lord was being properly represented. This included (1) insuring that the covenant was being kept by the people (so that God's holiness was appropriately represented), and (2) remaining a subordinate instrument for the Lord's military leadership and deliverances (so that God's kingship was appropriately represented).

The king had the responsibility to model adherence to the law—to serve as a model for Israel's conduct as well as to portray the God of Israel to the nations. When the king decided to lead the way in the worship of other gods, an unclear picture was given regarding whose divine kingship was being represented by that king. Was Yahweh king over all? Was Yahweh's kingship proclaimed over against the claims of other gods? With such questions it is easy to recognize that the failure of the king to obey the law and to be faithful to Yahweh jeopardized the clarity of God's self-revelation.[11] The biblical text indicates a continuing concern that the LORD be clearly portrayed as the leader of the armies of Israel. Incidents in which this is emphasized are many. From prophetic messages that the Lord will deliver the enemy into their hands (e.g., 2 Kings 3:18), to revelation of Yahweh's angelic hosts (2 Kings 6:17), to the forthright counsel of Isaiah to Ahaz and Hezekiah in their respective crises (Isa. 7–10; 2 Kings 19), Yahweh of hosts shows himself to be a formidable commander-in-chief. The obligation of human kings to subordinate their own strategies and rely on Yahweh is articulated specifically in Isaiah 7:9 where Ahaz is told that if he does not exercise this reliance on the Lord, he will not endure (the same verb is used to describe dynastic succession in the covenant).

> The political success or failure of a king was entirely dependent upon the degree to which Israel obeyed the covenant. Political success could thus only be achieved by a king through fulfilling his responsibility as covenant administrator. Given this view, it is also clear that military success was not a major accomplishment of a king, but the act of Yahweh in his role as protector of the people. The king's role in this was to trust Yahweh to deliver, and then to be obedient to his word. . . . In Israel the king was expected to

lead the people in covenant obedience and loyalty to
Yahweh. Then the king and the people could trust Yahweh
and rely upon him to bless them and deliver them from their
enemies as they lived in the land of milk and honey.[12]

When the text speaks of the nature of Saul's failure it says
that he did not keep the command of the Lord (1 Sam. 13:13–
14; 15:24). But this is not the same as failing to obey or uphold
the law. Gerbrandt has identified Saul's offenses in 1 Samuel
13 and 15 as improper conduct in holy war.

> In both chapters the central issue is then the king's obedience
> of Yahweh's word as communicated to him by the prophet
> Samuel. Saul had to learn through negative experience that
> although he had been appointed king, Yahweh was still
> responsible for the defence of the nation, and the king could
> not take affairs into his own hands. In Israel the king was
> expected to obey Yahweh in all areas, but this was especially
> important here since this was where the temptation was the
> greatest for the king to usurp Yahweh's position. In war and
> in defence of his people, Yahweh was king, and the human
> king was subservient to him.[13]

We have already seen that the matter of leading Israel's
armies into battle was of prime concern to the Israelites when
they requested a king, and was at the heart of their misunderstanding of the role of kingship. Despite the people's rejection
of Yahweh's military leadership, the text clearly identifies Saul
as having the potential of success even in the matter of leading
the armies in battle.

> Saul can save when he allows the spirit of God to act through
> him ([1 Sam.] 11:6). As 11:13 affirms, ultimately it is God who
> has wrought deliverance. . . . Kingship can be incorporated
> into Israel's structure and faith if it continues to allow
> Yahweh to be ultimately responsible for Israel's protection.[14]

The revelatory significance of this role of Yahweh can be clearly
seen in passages such as 1 Kings 20:13: "This is what the LORD
says: 'Do you see this vast army? I will give it into your hand
today, and then you will know that I am the LORD'" (see also
v. 28).

When Saul ceased to be a channel for Yahweh's protection and leadership, others were found who would respond appropriately as instruments of God's deliverance. Among these were Saul's son, Jonathan (1 Sam. 14), and David (1 Sam. 17). The latter continued to be portrayed as an appropriate vice-regent to Yahweh's military actions when he ascended the throne (2 Sam. 5:19–25).[15]

The Royal Psalms

In addition to the evidence from the historical literature, some information on this phase may also be gleaned from royal psalms such as Psalm 72. From the very beginning God is acknowledged as the source of the king's justice and righteousness. The psalm conveys throughout the function of the king and the hopes for the king. All of this is premised on his ability to operate in relationship to God. God's justice and righteousness are therefore being revealed when the king reigns with justice and righteousness. Likewise, Psalm 132 indicates a mutually supportive relationship between the Davidic dynasty in Jerusalem and Yahweh's kingship.[6] Thomas W. Mann has done a detailed study of the concept of the exaltation of the king (divine or human) as it occurs in biblical and ancient Near Eastern literature. Using Psalms 89 and 47, as well as the historical literature of 2 Samuel 5–7, he concludes that the exaltation of the Davidic dynasty is the principal means of presenting the exaltation of Yahweh as king.

> The victory of David over the Philistine oppression is described in terms directly related to the vanguard motif, which expresses Yahweh's presence in the conflict. The return of the sacred ark—itself an ancient representation of divine presence—to Israelite control, and, in fact, its processional journey to the newly established political capitol, Jerusalem, is the cultic correlate to the military triumph, and both together proclaim the exaltation of Yahweh and of David, the chosen king. The construction of the temple— first proposed under David, and fulfilled under Solomon—is the natural consummation of the rise of the Davidic empire. In the royal theology of the Solomonic era, the typology of

exaltation comes to full bloom in the person of the king, who is elevated above all others as the son of Yahweh, and whose kingdom is established forever. This near apotheosis of the royal figure, of course, has its counterpart in the exaltation of Yahweh, a process that began as early as the Exodus, but culminates in the Davidic period, when Yahweh fully incorporates the role of Elyon as the highest deity, and Yahweh's sovereignty extends to the nations surrounding the Davidic empire.[17]

Lexical Analysis

All of the above demonstrates the significance of Yahweh's kingship as a major motif in the literature pertaining to this period, but is there any lexical evidence that the king was understood as having the purpose of reflecting God's kingship? Such a case can be made through a lexical analysis of the phrase "Walk before (me)" (halak/hithalak liphne. . .).[18] The Qal (G) stem and Hithpael (HtD) stem occurrences may be considered together because there are related contexts that express the same meaning by using the variant form (cf., Qal usage in 1 Kings 9:4 and Hithpael usage in 2 Kings 20:3). The collocation of verb and preposition occurs nearly thirty times in a wide variety of contexts. These occurrences may be classified as follows:

1. People as Object of the Preposition

1. God as pillar of cloud *going before* Israel (Ex. 13:21; etc.) [G]
2. God *going before* Israel into the land (Deut. 1:30; 31:8) [G]
3. The Army *going before* the priests and the priests before the ark around Jericho (Josh. 6:9, 13) [G]
4. Used parallel to "rear guard" (Isa. 52:12; 58:8) [G]
5. The purpose of Jacob's gifts to Esau (Gen. 32:21) [G]
6. Actual role-conduct of Samuel (1 Sam. 12:2) [HtD]
7. Expected role-conduct of new priestly line ("before my anointed" 1 Sam. 2:35) [HtD]

2. God as Object of the Preposition

1. Expected role-conduct of Davidic kings (1 Kings 2:4; 8:23, 25; 9:4; 2 Chron. 6:16; 7:17) [G]
2. Actual role-conduct of Hezekiah (2 Kings 20:3; Isa. 38:3) [HtD]
3. Expected-actual role-conduct of the Patriarchs (Gen. 17:1; 24:40; 48:15) [HtD]
4. Expected role-conduct of priests (1 Sam. 2:30)[19] [HtD]
5. Anticipated role-conduct of psalmist who has been delivered (Pss. 56:13 [14]; 116:9) [HtD]

It is clear from the range of contexts in which this collocation of verb and preposition is used that it cannot be considered simply a synonym for keeping the law. Likewise the concepts of walking in full view of someone or enjoying someone's favor may suit a few of the contexts, but do not offer a unifying feature. When God walks before someone the most basic meanings appear to be guidance and protection. But when people are the subjects of the verb the contexts suggest that the meaning should be "to serve as an emissary."[20] This is appropriate to Samuel's role on behalf of the people and to the role of the priest and king on behalf of Yahweh. It is also appropriate to the priest's role on behalf of the king (1 Sam. 2:35). Even the guidance and protective functions of God can be encompassed by the function of emissary—in the sense that the emissary is considered a diplomatic vanguard.

The results of this lexical analysis suggest that one of the primary roles of the king was understood as being the emissary of King Yahweh. This was also an expectation of the Patriarchs. In both cases it is connected very closely to the covenant. This fact that the covenant-elect party of the covenant phase was to serve as emissary substantiates the revelatory role of election.

From Phase Two to Phase Three

Just as the book of Judges demonstrates the failure of the chosen people of God with regard to the Law, the books of Kings demonstrate the failures of the kings with regard to kingship. These failures cause the temporary loss of the elements gained in the previous two phases of development— their land and their status as an independent nation with their own king. Prior to this loss, however, prophets are already proclaiming that those benefits will eventually be restored in connection with a yet future phase of development that Jeremiah refers to as the new covenant. The continuity between this phase of development and the previous phases of the covenant as well as with the promises to Abraham can be easily documented in chapters 31–33 of Jeremiah. It is the law of phase one that the people will have in their hearts in this new phase of development (the new covenant), and this has an interesting side effect:

"No longer will a man teach his neighbor,
    or a man his brother, saying, 'Know the Lord,'
because they will all know me,
    from the least of them to the greatest." (Jer. 31:34; see
    also Hos. 2:20)

This appears to suggest that in this new phase of development the revelatory function of God's people will be obsolete. The only other information given is that God will forgive their sins. This suggests the provision of salvation from sins. Thus, in the initial proclamation of the phase known as the new covenant, it is signaled that the people of God will no longer have a revelatory function, and that God's forgiveness will be a primary feature. This conceptual shift had already begun in the remnant theology evident in classical prophecy—the faithful minority in Israel experiencing God's blessings.

Consequently, in some ways the events surrounding the return from exile constitute the close of the period during which Israel has served as the revelatory people of God. Though this function is phasing out, the promises associated with the covenant remain. Evidence for this includes the fact that the covenant promises continue to be affirmed in the aftermath oracles of even the postexilic prophets.

Though the Israelites are brought back to the land, the land is not restored to them, nor do they have their own king.

Therefore, the transitional period continues, its length having been delineated in Daniel's important oracles concerning four kingdoms and seventy weeks. We should note at this juncture that here the book of Esther makes its contribution, suggesting that God intends to continue to bless and deliver Israel, but that their function as his revelatory people has, for all intents and purposes, ceased. In some measure this is because the aim has been achieved (despite Israel's constant shortcomings). Evidence of this comes from an unexpected source. After Haman returned from leading Mordecai around the citadel of Susa in honor, Zeresh, Haman's wife, comments, "Since Mordecai, before whom your downfall has started, is of Jewish origin, you cannot stand against him—you will surely come to ruin!" (Esth. 6:13).

The third transitional period is spanned by the four kingdoms of Daniel, and covers the Exile, the postexilic period, and the intertestamental period. Although the next phase of development, the new covenant, has been proclaimed, it has not yet been realized. The next phase actually comes (and the transitional period ends) with the death and resurrection of Jesus.

In his lifetime Jesus embodied the revelatory aspects of the previous phases of development. As the Son of God he revealed God's character, and in so doing fulfilled the law and surpassed it, in which sense, the law was pointing to Christ.[21] As Messiah he revealed God's position, for he was God's King, a new Solomon (son of David), who would not fail to meet the qualifications and fulfill the conditions. This does not mean that the Sinai covenant or the Davidic covenant have been discarded or made obsolete. Rather, as revelatory instruments, they have been surpassed by a clearer revelation. Likewise, far from replacing the covenant promises made to Abraham, Jesus represents the climax of that covenant. The aspect of blessing has now become much clearer in Jesus.

The actual new phase of covenant development comes in the death and resurrection of Jesus because in them can be found the new elements of election and revelation. The new focus of election is that now believers in Christ constitute the elect and, as a result, are saved from their sin, as Jeremiah had prophesied. The shift from the third to the fourth phase of covenant development is now complete. The people of God, once comprised of ethnic Israel serving a revelatory function, is now comprised of believers, the heirs of salvation.

It should be understood, though, that these characterizations simply reflect primary emphases. Certainly the church can still perform a revelatory function (as can Israel), though God's program of special revelation is complete; and certainly there were those in ancient Israel whom we would consider to have been heirs of salvation. The question is: What is it that defined the people of God? In the model I am proposing the term "people of God" (in the Old Testament), defined those who served a revelatory function. Not all who served this function were necessarily saved. In contrast, the term "people of God" in the New Testament defined those who believed in Christ.

Theology has always struggled with the relationship between Israel and the church, for each is, in some way, considered to be the people of God. Since it is clear that not all Old Testament Israelites were believers, some theologians have therefore concluded that salvation in the Old Testament must have worked differently. Yet most have been uncomfortable with Israelites' being considered to be "saved" merely because of the circumstances of their birth, or by the circumcision that they received. This conundrum is easily enough resolved, however, by realizing that even though the church is considered the people of God by reason of its belief, the title is not necessarily attributed to Israel for the same purpose. When Israel entered into a covenant relationship with God they were not responding to a plan of salvation. They were not accepting redemption for their sins. Their covenant relationship with God was not intended to be soteric (i.e., providing salvation from sin). Referring to them as the people of God was not intended to address whether or not they were "saved." The status of the church as the people of God, on the other hand, is defined in precisely those terms—issues that will be discussed in further detail in chapters 7 and 8.

The new aspect of revelation that accompanies this stage of

development is, of course, the revelation of the plan of salvation—the presentation of God's provision of the means by which a relationship is permanently established. As Savior, Christ includes in his titles and functions this stage of development as well. In so doing, we can see that in the person of Jesus are encompassed both the elements of revelation (all the phases of revelation find their culmination in him) and of election (he represents the means by which salvation is provided).

EXCURSUS: THEOLOGY OF EXALTATION[22]

The whole series of covenant phases involving election, revelation, and salvation coheres in a theology of exaltation. When God chooses an individual or a corporate body, he exalts them. Their exaltation puts them on display as God's showcase for revealing his character and attributes. Through this process God himself is exalted. Even the lexical study done earlier draws these elements together. Yahweh exalts Israel by going before them (*halak liphne*) as a vanguard for protection and guidance. Likewise, the elect exalt Yahweh by walking before him, serving as his emissary.

The verb "to exalt" can be expressed by a number of different Hebrew verbs (*rwm*, *gdl*, and *ns'*). The terminology is significant first of all because it is more identifiable in the text than the terms election or revelation, and secondly because it can be applied appropriately to both parties in the covenant. "Elect" can apply to the human parties in the covenant but not to God. "Revelation" can apply to human parties revealing God, but not vice versa. In contrast, the various verbs for exalting can be used with either God or humans as subject or as object. Not only is the covenant relationship seen as exalting, but the inheriting of the promises is also exalting (Ps. 37:34).

The exaltation motif is not found specifically in the patriarchal narratives, though divine presence is expressed (e.g., Gen. 28:15). Nonetheless exaltation subtly enters the picture through the name Abram, "exalted father" and the fact that his name will be made great (Gen. 12:2). With the Exodus narratives the motif becomes more prominent, even though the text does not use any of the various verbs of exaltation to

describe Israel. Thomas Mann's study of Exodus 15 in light of
the ancient Near Eastern texts that feature exaltation shows that
a clear pattern exists.

> The combination of the motif of Israel's march along with
> those of divine presence in battle and the dominating theme
> of Yahweh's exaltation leads us to suggest a further, and
> more fundamental, resemblance between the Song and the
> Near Eastern texts. In the latter we frequently found that
> each major literary text examined, as well as the annals,
> reflected the institution or renaissance of an empire. We
> would assert that Exodus 15 not only uses many similar
> literary motifs, but is also proclaiming a very similar *Tendenz*.
> Simply put, it declares that Yahweh's exaltation is also the
> exaltation of Israel over Egypt and especially over the
> peoples of Palestine. Just as Tukulti-Ninurta was praised as
> the lord whom all kings dreaded, so it is claimed that Israel is
> the people before whom all the "enthroned of Canaan" melt
> in fear. Indeed, we can press the analogy even further: just
> as Tukulti-Ninurta's exaltation was couched in terms of
> quasi-divine birth, so Israel's exaltation is expressed in the
> Song through her special relationship to Yahweh who has
> "redeemed," in fact, "acquired" or "created" her.[23]

The use of exaltation typology is much more explicit with
regard to the Davidic dynasty. The exaltation of the king is
mentioned as early as Hannah's song (1 Sam. 2:10), figures
prominently in the dynastic understanding of David (2 Sam.
5:12; 22:47–49; 23:1; 1 Chron. 17:17; 29:25), and is replete
throughout the Psalms (see especially 89:19–29).

Finally, since Jesus is the finale of God's revelatory
program we expect also to see his exaltation. Peter's sermons in
the book of Acts include statements on the exaltation of Christ
to the right hand of God (2:33; 5:31). This exaltation is said to be
for the purpose of providing for repentance and forgiveness,
the very elements of the new covenant. Paul also speaks of the
exaltation of Jesus, particularly with regard to his name, which
reveals his character and nature.

Thus, throughout the revelatory program represented in
the covenant we find the election and exaltation of humans.

The resulting revelation in turn leads to the exaltation of God that takes place in the revelation of his attributes.

⁴In that day you will say:

> "Give thanks to the LORD, call on his name;
>   make known among the nations what he has done,
>   and proclaim that his name is exalted.
> ⁵Sing to the LORD, for he has done glorious things;
>   let this be known to all the world.
> ⁶Shout aloud and sing for joy, people of Zion,
>   for great is the Holy One of Israel among you."
> (Isa. 12:4–6)

In conclusion, the covenant is a revelatory program that operates by means of phases of election that are designed to highlight the nature and attributes of God. When God has made himself known in such a way, he closes the program of revelation by making a means of reconciliation possible through his son, Jesus Christ. The revelatory program thus eventuates in a soteric program. We have been given the knowledge of God so that we might enter into relationship with him. He has provided the revelation of himself and he has provided the way to himself—carried out so that God might be exalted.

NOTES

[1]By identifying this as fulfillment of the promise I am *not* suggesting that the land aspect of the covenant is no longer an issue or no longer in need of fulfillment.

[2]See A. F. Campbell, *The Ark Narrative* (Missoula: Scholars Press, 1975); and R. Polzin, *Samuel and the Deuteronomist* (San Francisco: Harper & Row, 1989), 64–71. See also Lyle Eslinger, *Kingship of God in Crisis* (Sheffield: Almond, 1985), 181: "It is not *because* the ark is lost that Israel experiences this blow to its leadership. Rather it is the corruption of the priestly leadership of Eli's sons that provokes Yahweh to arrange this defeat and to allow the loss of the ark." See also W. Dumbrell, *Covenant and Creation* (Nashville: Thomas Nelson, 1984), 133.

[3]Dumbrell, *Covenant and Creation*, 143–44.

[4]G. E. Gerbrandt, *Kingship According to the Deuteronomistic History* (Atlanta: Scholars Press, 1986), 148.

[5]V. P. Long, *The Reign and Rejection of King Saul* (Atlanta: Scholars Press, 1989), 90. On the other hand, M. Tsevat offers evidence of the fact that throughout the ancient Near East the king was understood to be the

representative or vice-regent of deity. Matitiahu Tsevat, "The Biblical Account of the Foundation of the Monarchy in Israel" in *The Meaning of the Book of Job and Other Biblical Studies* (New York: Ktav, 1980), 88–90.

[6]Matitiahu Tsevat, "The Biblical Account of the Foundation of the Monarchy in Israel," 91.

[7]See the discussion in V. P. Long, *The Reign and Rejection of King Saul*, 91–93. As cited by Long, this understanding of the phrase traditionally rendered "a man after God's own heart" has been defended by P. K. McCarter, *1 Samuel* (Garden City: Anchor, 1980), 229, and is further supported by comparative Semitics.

[8]A. R. Johnson, *Sacral Kingship In Ancient Israel* (Cardiff: University of Wales, 1955), 14.

[9]Cf., B. Childs, *Introduction to the Old Testament as Scripture* (Philadelphia: Fortress, 1979), 272–73; W. J. Dumbrell, "The Content and Significance of the Books of Samuel: Their Place and Purpose within the Former Prophets" *JETS* 33 (1990), 51; J. T. Willis, "The Song of Hannah and Psalm 113" *CBQ* 34 (1973), 139–54; R. Polzin, *Samuel and the Deuteronomist*, 31–36.

[10]G. E. Gerbrandt *Kingship According to the Deuteronomistic History*, 99.

[11]Ibid., 177–80.

[12]Ibid., 194.

[13]Ibid., 157.

[14]Ibid., 153.

[15]Ibid., 171. Especially, "Thus Yahweh could use David, not because he was a great military leader, but because he was faithful. In this way a good king can be an agent by which the people are blessed." And I would add, by which God's kingship can be revealed, though that is not Gerbrandt's emphasis.

[16]T. Fretheim, "Psalm 132: A Form-Critical Study" *JBL* 86 (1967): 289–300.

[17]T. W. Mann, *Divine Presence and Guidance in Israelite Traditions: The Typology of Exaltation* (Baltimore: Johns Hopkins, 1977), 224. See also J. J. M. Roberts, "The Davidic Origin of the Zion Tradition" *JBL* 92 (1973): 329–44; and "The Religio-Political Setting of Psalm 47" *BASOR* 221 (1976): 129–32.

[18]This phrase is analyzed in *TDOT* III:392–93 but with very different results. The analysis there does not succeed in identifying the common ground that unites the lexeme across its semantic range, nor does it substantiate its subjective findings.

[19]This verse is typically translated in terms of an appointment that God had made (e.g., NIV: "I promised that your house and your father's house would *minister before me* forever. But now the Lord declares: Far be it from me!") But nowhere else is this collocation speaking of what the Lord grants or takes away. Instead it should be translated here as modal, i.e., " I clearly said that your house and your father's house *should* walk before me forever." It refers to what was expected of them instead of what was granted to them. This makes much better sense of the oracle and has the added advantage of avoiding the perception that God is going back on a promise. The modal aspect of the

imperfect is well recognized in the grammars (Waltke and O'Connor, 31.4g; GKC, 107 m–n).

[20]M. Weinfeld relates this expression to 'amad liphne but does so without explanation or defense. See M. Weinfeld, "The Covenant of Grant in the Old Testament and in the Ancient Near East" *JAOS* 90 (1970): 186n.19.

[21]Cf. the following statement by R. Badenas, *Christ the End of the Law* (Sheffield: JSOT Press, 1985): 150–51: "In the light of such an encompassing understanding of the Torah-Christ relation, it is not difficult to see why the simple fulfillment of historical predictions seems to be less important to Paul than to other NT writers. Even the broader fulfillment of types seems to him of secondary importance. For Paul the relation of the OT to Christ is much deeper and more consistent than that. Its structure cannot be reduced to the categories of prediction-fulfillment or typology. Paul expresses it in a category more basic and comprehensive than these, namely, in the teleological category of purpose and realization. Since Paul saw Christ as the end toward which the law was directed, it may be deduced that Christ took the place of the centrality of the law in Paul's life, but that Paul's respect for the law remained the same (Rom. 3.31; 7.12, 14). However, Paul's veneration for the law was surpassed by his veneration for Christ. This surpassing of Torah by Christ is what Paul wished to teach Israel and this is what Israel did not accept. As a corollary to Paul's understanding of the law in the light of Christ, it follows that he could not view the law any more as an end in itself but as a means. Precisely what Paul reproached the Jews for was their looking at the law as a goal in itself (9.31–32); they did not see that it pointed and led to Christ (10.4)."

[22]For the direction of this section I am heavily indebted to the work of Thomas Mann, *Divine Presence and Guidance in Israelite Traditions*.

[23]Ibid., 129–30.

5

PARALLELS BETWEEN THE COVENANT PHASES

The scheme of history presented in the last chapter suggests that there may be parallels that exist between the phases of covenant development, and in this chapter we will explore the extent of those parallels. The interest lies not in parallels between the covenants themselves, but in the events involved in their respective phases. These identified parallels lie between the Mosaic and Davidic phases and, on a more limited scale, between the Abrahamic and new covenant phases.

PARALLELS BETWEEN THE MOSAIC AND DAVIDIC PHASES

The chart on the next page displays the general movement of the narratives and serves as the guide for our analysis.

Covenant Phase Inaugurated

It should immediately be observed that there is a significant difference between the Mosaic and the Davidic covenant phases in regard to their inauguration. The Mosaic covenant phase was initiated by God when he brought the Israelites to Mount Sinai for the giving of the Law. The Davidic covenant phase was initiated by the people when they demanded a king. Nevertheless, God used both beginnings to embark on a new development in the progress of revelation. Though the people initiated the Davidic phase in the sense that

82

they asked for a king, God already had initiated the transition from the Mosaic phase to a new phase when he indicted and judged the priesthood (1 Sam. 2–3), and when he brought Samuel into place to preside over the inauguration of the new phase. It should further be noted that God's kingship is revealed as much by Saul's failure as by David's success. The contrast is instrumental in the revelation.

NARRATIVE ELEMENTS	LAW (Mosaic)	KINGSHIP (Davidic)
Covenant phase inaugurated	Giving of the law Golden calf	Anointing of a king: Saul
Initial jeopardy	Golden calf	Saul's failure to act
First-generation failure	Wilderness	Saul's reign
Successful inauguration	Deuteronomy	Davidic covenant
Long-term failure	Judges period	Monarchy period

Similarities exist in that both phases include the laying down of ordinances in a book. In Exodus 24:3 (cf. v. 7) the ordinances (*mišpaṭim*) represent the law (all the words of Yahweh). Less obvious, in 1 Samuel 10:25 the ordinance (*mišpaṭ*) of the kingdom is written in a book before the people. The comparability of this document to the law is evident in Matitiahu Tsevat's analysis of its purpose.

> Not privileges but obligation and limitation are the substance of "the rule of the king" or "the rule of kingship" that is written down in a document and deposited before God. The limitation is that their king is not to be like the kings of all the nations, and, consequently, Israel is not to be a nation like all the nations. The authority of the king does not originate in him or the people but in God; he is God's deputy and viceregent.[1]

A further parallel is found in the eating of a ceremonial meal by the parties involved in the inauguration (Ex. 24:11; 1 Sam. 9:24). Additionally we should not lose sight of the fact that both of these phases are preceded by mighty acts of deliverance by Yahweh. The ten plagues and the Exodus are well recognized as such, while the exodus of the ark from Philistia is developed

in parallel terms by the literary presentation of the author of
1 Samuel 4–6.[2]

Initial Jeopardy

In the Mosaic phase the law was no sooner given (Moses is
not yet down from the mountain) than the whole operation was
jeopardized by a major violation of the law on the part of the
people. As is clear in the conversations between God and
Moses, the jeopardy was so great that God considered destroying the people and starting over again with Moses. When
Moses viewed the scene at the bottom of the mountain he broke
the tablets. The result was that the tablets had to be made
again, giving a stutter-step appearance to the initiation process.

In the Davidic phase the people's request itself is wrong-
headed because it is premised on an incorrect concept of
kingship. Nonetheless, Saul is chosen and is anointed and
commissioned by Samuel. The true jeopardy to this phase is
seen in Saul's failure to act in his new capacity as king. V.
Philips Long has suggested that a careful reading of 1 Samuel
9–10 shows that when Samuel instructed Saul to "do whatever
your hand finds to do," after he had met up with the prophets
near the tree of Tabor (10:7–8), that Samuel intended for Saul to
attack the Philistine garrison at Gibeah.[3]

Instead, Saul simply went home, and in so doing, jeopardized the whole process. It is not until Saul initiated the victory
against the Ammonites that the covenant process got back on
track and, at that point, the kingdom was "renewed" (11:14,
NIV: "reaffirmed").

> How then are we to understand the "renewal" of the
> kingdom? In what sense is it possible to speak of Saul's
> kingdom in a state of deterioration and in need of renewal?
> Again, we must recall our discussion of the anointing
> episode. There we argued that Saul's anointing and its
> confirmation by three signs should have been followed by an
> act of provocation against the Philistines. Such an action
> would have brought Saul to public attention by demonstrat-
> ing his abilities as a deliverer. In a manner not inconsistent
> with his character as depicted elsewhere, however, Saul

hesitated to "do what his hand found to do" (cf., 10:7), and
the accession process was, temporarily at least, arrested. In
the absence of any demonstration of his saving abilities, even
Saul's selection by lot and his commanding physique were
insufficient to gain him the unanimous support of the people
(cf., 10:27). Finally, the Ammonite victory, though not *the*
demonstration envisaged at the time of Saul's anointing and
commissioning, was sufficient to silence the dissenters and
set the accession process back on track.[4]

Thus, as in the case of the inauguration of the law,
kingship was immediately put in jeopardy by failure in the
foundational element, and the subsequent need for re-inaugu-
ration follows in the same stutter-step pattern. Both of these
initial jeopardies resulted in covenant renewals. In Exodus 32–
33 Moses went back up the mountain and received a second
copy of the Law. In 1 Samuel 11 there is a "renewal of the
kingdom."

Not only is a renewal of the monarchy possible in the
context of chapters 10 [and following], but it is absolutely
necessary as an opportunity for the people to affirm their
acceptance of and allegiance to the monarchy offered to them
by Yahweh. The renewal will mark the beginning of a new
period in Israelite political history in which the people are
willingly governed by a king given to them by Yahweh on
the express condition that the theocracy remains, with the
king ruling only as Yahweh's designate. The renewal gives
the people the chance to say yes to this condition with the
unambiguous and unanimous affirmation, not previously
given.[5]

First Generation Failure

In the Mosaic phase the failure of the first generation came
in its refusal to enter the land of Canaan. Though God was
willing and able to bring them into the land and drive out the
inhabitants, the people were fearful and would not trust the
Lord (Num. 13–14). Consequently the Lord came to the brink
of destroying them and choosing another people for himself
(Num. 14:12). Moses interceded on their behalf and they were

not destroyed, but God made it clear that he had rejected that generation because they had turned back from following the Lord (Num. 14:42–43). This in turn led to a forty-year postponement of God's intention to give them the land. During this time the ark of the covenant was apparently kept outside the camp (Ex. 33:1–6). It was a period of great frustration for Moses, who had to tolerate constant grumbling and frequent rebellion.

In the Davidic phase the general pattern is very similar. Here the failure of Saul's kingship quickly becomes evident. If the assignment of forty years to Saul's reign is accurate, even the time span is similar to Israel's wilderness experience. As in the case with the wilderness generation, God expressed that he had been willing to bring success, but Saul's failure led instead to rejection and God's choosing another (1 Sam. 13:13–14). Again we find that the ark of the covenant is "outside the camp" (in Kiriath-jearim), and the prophet Samuel struggled in frustration through this now-aborted start. Like Moses, he died not seeing the actual inauguration, though he, also like Moses, designated the one who would bring it about.[6]

In addition to the similarities in the major progression of events, there are also some intriguing parallels in the minor details. For example, the failure of the Israelites to enter the land of Canaan is followed immediately by a challenge to the priestly office of Moses (Korah's rebellion, Num. 16). Similarly, it is a usurpation of Samuel's priestly office that serves as the occasion for the initial rejection of Saul (1 Sam. 13). In each case the incident is followed by the designation of a clan and tribe through which God is going to work. The Levites are set apart in Numbers 18:1–7, while the tribe of Judah represents God's choice for the next king. Jeremiah makes explicit comments showing his understanding of the similarities between the elect status of these two houses (33:24).

As another example, in both Numbers and Samuel, there are attempts to impede God's plan to carry out his intention, and both lead to the antagonist's prophesying against his will. Balaam attempted to hinder Israel's movement toward Canaan (Num. 22), and Saul attempted to kill David while he was staying with Samuel, but ended up helplessly entranced (1 Sam. 19:18–24). Just as Balaam uttered four prophecies, so Saul's three groups of messengers, then he, himself, fell into prophetic trances. Even the Amalekites serve as a parallel in that Saul's military activity against them is in response to their aggression against the wilderness generation (1 Sam. 15:2). These are all minor elements, however, and are simply added attractions to the main correlations. One must be cautious lest imagination dives in where evidence fears to tread.

With all of this it must be acknowledged that some significant differences also exist. Most prominent is the fact that during this entire sequence in the Mosaic phase, the covenant had already been presented and ratified. In the Davidic phase, however, there was no hint of a covenant until David came to the throne. Nonetheless, the parallels identified above provide a basis for comparison even though the phases do not correspond at every point. The lack of exact correspondence may even help to show that these parallels represent a historigraphical-theological interpretation on the part of the editors of Scripture rather than an artificial grid that makes history conform to their pattern.

Successful Inauguration

After a one-generation postponement the book of Deuteronomy represents the presentation of the law to a generation that is now ready to enter the land successfully and fulfill the election that had been aborted by the previous generation. With acceptance of the law and trust in the Lord, this second generation conquered the land. Joshua's leadership was godly and the people were faithful during his days (Josh. 24:31). The ark of the covenant was reestablished as central and served a pivotal role as the representation of God's presence in their midst.

In the Davidic phase the successful reinauguration is found in the establishment of the Davidic covenant. As in the time of Joshua, David was able to establish control of the land, and thus inherits one of the covenant blessings promised to Abraham. Likewise, as in the time of Joshua, the ark was brought into prominence as David installed it in his newly conquered capital city. Terence Fretheim identified this parallel in his analysis of Psalm 132:

> The ark processional is related to the motif of Yahweh's leading his people through the wilderness and into the promised land. . . . It is only when Yahweh finds his place in Zion that rest comes from the enemies round about.[7]

Occupation of Land

In both the Mosaic and the Davidic phases the conquest of the land leads to an occupation of the land according to the covenant promises that God made to Abraham. This serves as God's pledge of good faith. Since the inauguration has now successfully taken place, God shows his faithfulness by providing that which was promised.

Second Generation Jeopardy

In the Mosaic phase the people of Israel conquered the land and occupied it, but as Joshua and Judges both make clear, they failed to drive out the inhabitants. The law phase was based on the premise, "You are to be holy, because I, the LORD your God, am holy." The law everywhere recognized that if the Canaanites were not driven out of the land, the Israelites' ability to achieve holiness would be severely compromised. The holiness of God would be less evident if his people were not holy. Thus the covenant was no sooner inaugurated than it was placed in jeopardy. When the Israelites failed to abide by the law, the revelatory picture became clouded. Their failure to drive out the inhabitants jeopardized not only the revelation aspect of the covenant, but also the blessings aspect. And so Israel's possession of the land was constantly threatened.

In the Davidic phase, the second-generation jeopardy came in David's family problems. Just as the revelation of God's holiness was compromised by Israel's inability to mirror holiness in their society in the Mosaic phase, so the revelation of God's kingship was compromised by David's and his sons' abuse of power. This becomes the theme of the second part of

2 Samuel. Clearest evidence for this is that though the Uriah and Bathsheba incident specifically involved adultery and murder, the judgment of God through Nathan puts the emphasis squarely on the abuse of power.[8] This abuse continued in his sons, Amnon, Absalom, Adonijah, and Solomon, bringing jeopardy to David's line and leading eventually to significant territorial loss. Further discussion of the motif of covenant jeopardy and its implications will be reserved for the next chapter.

Long-Term Failure

The four hundred years of the period of the judges demonstrated the long-term failure of Israel with regard to the Mosaic phase. It showed how the law was neglected (the people worshiped Baal and did what was right in their own eyes). Yet the four hundred years also showed how God continued to demonstrate his holiness by his dealings with Israel. The narrator's formulas used in presenting the cycles give evidence that it was precisely this issue that is the central agenda. The people failed to follow the law and the resulting cycles show God's holiness, sovereignty, justice, and grace. Thus God's revelatory program moves forward despite the failures of the people. God's revelation of himself takes place in his dealings with his recalcitrant people rather than in the way that they reflect his holiness in their conduct.

The Davidic phase likewise contains about four hundred years of history showing the long-term failure of the Israelite monarchy regarding the issue of kingship. The narrator's formulas again show that this is the agenda of the books of Kings when they make constant reference to Israel's walking in the sins of Jeroboam or not walking in the ways of David. Again, however, though the kings of Israel and Judah failed to represent God's kingship adequately, and in the process jeopardized the covenant blessings, throughout their history, God constantly revealed himself as king through his active role in their history. Thus, the Lord led them in battle and established justice, many times through the instrumentality of the prophets (cf., especially Elisha, see chapter 6 for further discussion).

Each of these long-term failures led eventually into periods of transition—the self-imposed exile of the ark following the Mosaic phase, and the Exile of the people following the Davidic phase. Each phase ended in the destruction of the primary center of the cultic worship of its time (Shiloh and Jerusalem respectively), and in the disintegration of the institutional backbone of the period (priesthood and kingship respectively). Jeremiah recognized the parallels when he threatened Jerusalem with the fate of Shiloh (Jer. 7:12–14; 26:6).

PARALLELS BETWEEN ABRAHAMIC AND NEW COVENANT PHASES

From the above analysis it is an easy matter to conclude that parallels exist in at least the broad scope of the course of events surrounding the Mosaic and Davidic phases of covenant development. While these structural parallels do not extend to the Abrahamic and new covenant phases, and structural similarities have not been identified between the Abrahamic and new covenant phases, there are, nevertheless, certain similarities between these two latter phases that should not be overlooked. Both phases have to cope with harsh reality: Can God's plan be implemented? In each phase a crucial element is missing without which the program cannot proceed. In the Abrahamic phase nothing can happen if Abraham does not have a son. In the new covenant phase the Jews are awaiting the appearance of God's Messiah, the Davidic king, to preside over the restoration. Both phases require the appearance of an individual. Likewise both phases struggle with similar issues regarding that individual.

Whose Son Is He?

In the Abrahamic phase this question arises in several different ways. At first the thought of an adopted son (Lot or Eliezer) seemed appropriate until Abraham was informed that his own son would be his heir. Then Ishmael was born with Abraham's expectation that he was the promised son, though he was not Sarah's. This state of affairs continued for thirteen years until it was announced that Sarah herself would give birth to the heir. Even after this announcement there was a problem because after Sarah had been taken into the harem of Abimelek of Gerar the possibility arose that the child she would bear could have been conceived by someone other than Abraham. Thus, the suspenseful chapters of the patriarchal narratives revolve around the issue of sonship.

Likewise, when Jesus comes to inaugurate the new covenant phase of God's program, the issue of sonship is at the center of the controversy in a number of ways. First of all his human lineage is of extreme importance. Two of the Gospels offer genealogies and numerous other evidences are presented to show him to be of the house and lineage of David. This is, of course, essential to any Messianic claim. Secondly, Jesus' divine sonship is very much an issue. The Jews of the first century were not unused to individuals being acclaimed as the Messiah. It is when Jesus identified himself more closely with God that he drew the indignation of the Jewish leaders. Even the title Son of God was ambiguous enough so that it could be tolerated (all people of faith were, in a sense, God's children), and it may have been included in the credentials of the Messiah as early as the Qumran literature.[9] But when Jesus explained his Sonship as comprised of oneness with the Father, his enemies pushed their accusations past megalomania to blasphemy. Thirdly, and not unrelated to the other two, the doctrine of the Virgin Birth also focuses attention on the issue of sonship.

How Can the Promise Be Fulfilled If He Is Dead?

After the tension of the Abrahamic narratives has been resolved and Isaac is safely in place as heir to the covenant promises, a situation suddenly arises that throws everything back into confusion—God instructs Abraham to sacrifice Isaac. Throughout centuries of interpretation it has been commonplace for allegories and typologies to be constructed between this event and the crucifixion of Christ. While it is not our intention to revive such hermeneutical contortions of the past, there is the issue of parallel motifs to be considered. The recurring motif is, of course, that the death of the principal party (i.e., Isaac and Jesus) has the appearance of making the covenant promises impossible to fulfill. This issue will be further explored in chapter six's discussion of covenant jeopardy.

CONCLUSIONS

The parallels that have been identified in this chapter are admittedly secondary. That is, there is no evidence by which to suggest that the authors of Scripture were aware of them or crafted the narratives to highlight them. If this is so, what significance do they have? If these parallels are only the result of interpretive insight (ancient or modern), there would be no compositional implications. Though I have not been able to find any direct statements in Samuel or Kings that would suggest that the author(s) were aware of the parallels, it must be remembered that the authors of Scripture rarely offer forthright explanations of their literary purposes and methods. More often we can infer purpose by observations of selection, arrangement, and emphasis. On that count I must admit that I find it difficult to believe that such an extent of similarity could exist without the author's being aware of it. This is certainly an area for continued research, for if it could be demonstrated that the authors were aware of the parallels, our view of the composition of the deuteronomistic history and the Pentateuch would be revolutionized.

NOTES

[1]Matitiahu Tsevat, "The Biblical Account of the Foundation of the Monarchy in Israel" in *The Meaning of the Book of Job and Other Biblical Studies* (New York: Ktav, 1980), 86–87.

[2]See Lyle Eslinger, *Kingship of God in Crisis* (Sheffield: Almond, 1985), 199–201, and additional bibliography that he cites.

[3]V. P. Long, *The Reign and Rejection of King Saul* (Atlanta: Scholars Press, 1989), 51. This is to some extent also recognized in R. Polzin, *Samuel and the Deuteronomist* (San Francisco: Harper & Row, 1989), 106–7.

[4]V. P. Long, *The Reign and Rejection of King Saul*, 227–28.

[5]Lyle Eslinger, *Kingship of God in Crisis*, 379.

⁶Other similarities between Moses and Samuel exist including their initial reluctance to play their designated roles (Ex. 3, 1 Sam. 8) and their inclination toward usurping God's glory (Num. 12, 1 Sam. 12). For perhaps an overdone analysis of Samuel's weaknesses see R. Polzin, *Samuel and the Deuteronomist*.

⁷T. Fretheim, "Psalm 132: A Form-Critical Study" *JBL* 86 (1967): 300.

⁸See R. Westbrook, *Studies in Biblical and Cuneiform Law*, (Paris: J. Gabalda, 1988), 30–35.

⁹Cf. 4Q246 (Son of God Text) In Aramaic: "He shall be called the Son of God; they will call him Son of the Most High . . . He will judge the earth in righteousness . . . and every nation will bow down to him . . . with (God's) help he will make war, and . . . [God] will give all the peoples into his power." Michael Wise and James Tabor, "The Messiah at Qumran" *BAR* 18.6 (1992): 61. For a detailed discussion of the text and interpretive options see Joseph Fitzmyer, "4Q246: The 'Son of God' Document from Qumran" *Biblica* 62 (1993): 153–74.

6

THE MOTIF
OF COVENANT JEOPARDY

WHAT IS IN JEOPARDY?

Covenant jeopardy occurs when a situation develops in which one of the parties of the covenant fails to fulfill what the covenant calls him to do or when it appears unlikely that the agreement will be honored. In regard to the covenant between God and Israel, jeopardy could possibly occur on God's side if he failed to deliver on his promises. As for Israel (or Abraham or David), the covenant could be jeopardized by their failing to obey or failing to fulfill the law, etc. Covenant jeopardy, however, does not always mean that the covenant has been broken or defaulted on or that the covenant relationship ends, though at times any of these may be possibilities.

In order to provide a textual basis for this discussion of covenant jeopardy it is necessary to review some of the terminology that is used when the Old Testament speaks of jeopardy to the covenant. The two most familiar verbs associated with jeopardy are *'abar* and *heper* (hiphil of the root *prr*), both occurring with covenant (*berit*) as direct objects. Other nouns that serve as direct objects of these verbs are "commandments" and "law." The verb *'abar* occurs nine times with regard to the covenant, and is used to express a violation of the terms of the covenant. It was possible for an individual to violate the covenant by worshiping other gods (Josh. 23:16; Judg. 2:20), by rebelling against the law (Hos. 8:1), or by neglecting specific instructions (e.g., the ban, Josh. 7:11, 15). Violation of the covenant is cited as the cause of the deportation of the northern kingdom of Israel (2 Kings 18:12) and the fall of Jerusalem (Jer. 34:18).

The second verb (*heper*) is more frequent, more significant, and more controversial. It is often translated "nullify" primarily on the strength of its use with covenants and/or treaties and vows (Num. 30). The verb occurs just over fifty times, mostly in the hiphil, with nearly half the occurrences in covenant contexts. Though the collocation with *berit* is common, it does not appear to be idiomatic. Therefore it is important to explore the other collocations in order to nuance the verb correctly. The nouns that can be subjected to this verbal activity are: plans (Job 5:12; Prov. 15:22), vows (Num. 30:8–13), counsel or advice (2 Sam. 15:34; 17:14; Ps. 33:10; Neh. 4:15; Isa. 14:27), piety (Job 15:4), God's justice (Job 40:8), God's anger (Ps. 85:5), and the signs of the false prophets (Isa. 44:25). As one looks at this collection of objects and the circumstances that shape each of the verbal situations, it becomes clear that the English translation "nullify" does not quite provide the solution, if, as is usually the case, it means "to annul," as in a legal sense. If something is annulled, it legally never existed. In contrast, the nuance required by these contexts is to cause something to be of no effect, or to undermine the purpose or effect of something. When advice or counsel or plans are *heper* they do not achieve their intent or purpose. They are rendered ineffectual. The same is true of God's justice in Job 40:8 and of God's anger in Psalm 85:5. This nuance is likewise appropriate to the more ritualized contexts of vows and the signs of false prophets. Both can be rendered ritually ineffectual.

When this nuance is applied to the covenant contexts, important insights emerge. Forsaking Yahweh and worshiping idols can render the covenant ineffectual (Deut. 31:16, 20; Jer. 11:10). This does not mean that the covenant is null and void, but that it is rendered ineffectual in terms of its intended purpose. More significant are the three passages in which God is the subject of the verb.

⁴³For the land will be deserted by them and will enjoy its sabbaths while it lies desolate without them. They will pay for their sins because they rejected my laws and abhorred my decrees. ⁴⁴Yet in spite of this, when they are in the land of their enemies, I will not reject them or abhor them so as to destroy them completely, *breaking* my covenant with them. I am the LORD their God. ⁴⁵But for their sake I will remember the covenant with their ancestors whom I brought out of Egypt in the sight of the nations to be their God. I am the LORD. (Lev. 26:43–45; italics mine)

¹The angel of the LORD went up from Gilgal to Bokim and said, "I brought you up out of Egypt and led you into the land that I swore to give to your forefathers. I said, 'I will never *break* my covenant with you.' "(Judg. 2:1; italics mine)

> ¹⁹Have you rejected Judah completely?
>   Do you despise Zion?
> Why have you afflicted us
>   so that we cannot be healed?
> We hoped for peace
>   but no good has come,
> for a time of healing
>   but there is only terror.
> ²⁰O LORD, we acknowledge our wickedness
>   and the guilt of our fathers;
>   we have indeed sinned against you.
> ²¹For the sake of your name do not despise us;
>   do not dishonor your glorious throne.
> Remember your covenant with us
>   and do not *break* it. (Jer. 14:19–21; italics mine)

It will be noticed that the NIV translates *heper* as "to break." It is clear in two of these contexts that God would *heper* the covenant, if he decided to reject Israel. Here again, the issue cannot be God's breaking the covenant by violating the terms of it, nor do the contexts suggest a legal annulment. Rather, the most suitable common denominator is the translation, "to render ineffectual." My conclusion is that this verb is used to convey that the covenant's *purpose* is being jeopardized or negated, not its *existence*.

We must ask, then, which elements of the covenant can be

jeopardized. If we accept that God has determined to reveal himself, and that he has chosen to do so by means of a series of covenant phases, then our belief in the sovereignty of God would suggest that his self-revelation cannot be jeopardized. Nothing can prevent God from revealing himself. It can only be a matter of whether that program of revelation is carried out with Israel's cooperation or without it.

Consequently, both logic and Scripture clearly indicate that Israel's potential to benefit from the covenant relationship could be jeopardized. If they are not cooperative, if they do not keep the law, if they do not conduct themselves as God's people ought, they will be in danger of losing the land and their national identity. This may be termed *benefit jeopardy*. It is most clearly seen in the cursing sections of the covenant (Lev. 26:14–30; Deut. 28:15–68) and in the conditional clauses attached to the Davidic phase (1 Kings 9:6–9). This benefit jeopardy applies to the uncooperative generation(s).

There is, nevertheless, a class of jeopardy that is more foundational. Failure on the part of the human party prior to or soon after ratification could jeopardize their involvement in that phase of the covenant. If Abraham had not left his home and family to go to the land God showed him, the covenant would not have been made with him. When Israel made a golden calf to worship while Moses was on Mount Sinai, God spoke of destroying them and starting with another subgroup (Moses' line). This type of jeopardy has the potential to abort the covenant relationship before it is established and may be referred to as *abortive jeopardy*.

A third area of jeopardy concerns how God will be able to carry out his end of the agreement given the various circumstances that arise other than human failures, stubbornness, etc. (e.g., Abraham and Sarah's childlessness; Canaanite occupation of the land). In these instances there has been no failure on God's part. A sense of jeopardy is created by the fact that only a supernatural intervention could alleviate the situation. The stumbling blocks seem insurmountable and the result may be called *circumstantial jeopardy*.

A final class of jeopardy is related to benefit jeopardy.

STRUCTURE OF GENESIS 12-22

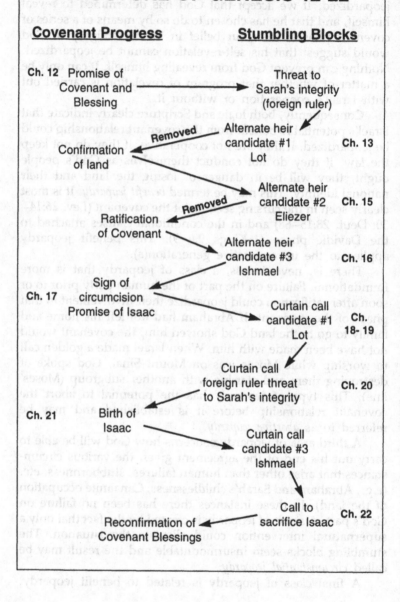

Covenant Progress

Stumbling Blocks

Ch. 12 Promise of
Covenant and ──────▶ Threat to
Blessing Sarah's integrity
(foreign ruler)

Removed Alternate heir
Confirmation candidate #1 Ch. 13
of land Lot

Alternate heir
Removed candidate #2 Ch. 15
Ratification Eliezer
of Covenant
Alternate heir
candidate #3 Ch. 16
Ishmael

Sign of
Ch. 17 circumcision
Promise of Isaac Curtain call
candidate #1 Ch.
Lot 18-19

Curtain call
foreign ruler threat Ch. 20
to Sarah's integrity

Ch. 21 Birth of
Isaac
Curtain call
candidate #3
Ishmael

Call to
Reconfirmation of ◀──── sacrifice Isaac Ch. 22
Covenant Blessings

When human failure reaches a level that clouds God's revelation, not only are the benefits in jeopardy, but God's program of self-revelation must pursue an alternate route in order to be carried out. This may be called *revelation jeopardy*. Notwithstanding, it should be understood that God's program is never in doubt. It is just that when humans fail to cooperate, God chooses alternate means by which the revelation will take place, often at the expense of the uncooperative party. As we examine each phase of the covenant we will attempt to identify which types of jeopardy exist and how the jeopardy is resolved.

JEOPARDY IN THE ABRAHAMIC PHASE

In the book of Genesis the entire framework of the narrative is built on the issue of covenant jeopardy. From Sarah's barrenness to the wife-sister accounts, from competing heirs to the near loss of the promised heir, from sibling rivalry to leaving the land, the patriarchal narratives are driven by covenant jeopardy. Indeed the selection, arrangement, and emphasis within the material suggest that covenant jeopardy is used by the author to reveal Yahweh as a God who is so determined and faithful that no circumstances can deter him from carrying out his purposes.

The structure of Genesis 12–22 is built on successive cycles of jeopardy and resolution (see chart on p. 98).[1] There is a slight degree of abortive jeopardy allowed for in regard to Abram's willingness to go to the land that God intended to show him. Otherwise the narratives are carried by circumstantial jeopardy. If Abraham has no children, how can God carry out his promises? If Isaac is sacrificed, how can the promises of God be fulfilled in him? In such cases of circumstantial jeopardy God reveals his sovereignty and intervenes with supernatural acts. Thus the jeopardy provides an opportunity for part of the revelation. Yahweh's sovereignty knows no obstacles.

As the generations continue, so does the jeopardy. Both Rebekah and Rachel are barren as was Sarah, thus, the line is in constant danger of extinction. Abraham shows a sense of his awareness of the jeopardy when he forbids Isaac to leave the land (Gen. 24:6–7). Jeopardy continues in the rivalry between

Esau and Jacob, in Jacob's leaving the land to live with Laban, and in the migration of the entire clan to Egypt. All of this is circumstantial jeopardy for it concerns God's ability to overcome obstacles and still fulfill his promises.

The resolution of most of the patriarchal jeopardy comes in the books of Exodus through Joshua when it becomes clear that Israel has become a great people and God takes his people back into the land that had been promised to them.

JEOPARDY IN THE MOSAIC PHASE

In the Mosaic phase of the covenant the jeopardy concerns the people's willingness to be cooperative in the revelation program. The law is a means of revealing what God is like. If the people do not remain loyal to the Lord and do not reflect his holiness in their way of life, God's program of revelation is jeopardized because God's name is profaned. If they refuse to allow him to take them into the land, he is not able to reveal his sovereignty, and the people are not able to benefit from the promised blessings. In the end, however, all that is in question is whether God will be revealed through Israel's faithful reflection of him, or whether he will reveal himself through his discipline of Israel's unfaithfulness. (Notice in the book of Ezekiel that revelation is the theme of Israel's judgment: "When I punish you, then you/the nations will know that I am the Lord"). God's self-revelation *will* be accomplished through Israel, one way or another.

The Exodus narratives begin with circumstantial jeopardy. Israel is in slavery in Egypt and the Egyptians are not inclined to release them. Yahweh's supernatural acts (the plagues and the parting of the sea) reveal his power, provide redemption from slavery, and bring resolution to the jeopardy. The giving of the law at Sinai is characterized by abortive jeopardy. Israel nearly disqualifies itself by worshiping the golden calf, but the jeopardy is resolved through the intervention of Moses. Benefit jeopardy occurs when the Israelites fear the occupants of the land and doubt Yahweh's ability to give them possession of the land. As a result the wilderness generation loses the benefit of the land—they die in the wilderness.

Throughout the subsequent Judges period there is benefit jeopardy. Since the Israelites did not drive out the inhabitants of the land as they had been instructed to do, they did not enjoy unhindered possession of the land. Furthermore, their incessant failure to obey the law and be faithful to Yahweh led to continuing oppression by enemies.

Because of Israel's continual violation of the law, there was also revelation jeopardy. How was God's character to be revealed if his people did not serve as a channel for that revelation? During the Judges period we find that God reveals his character through his ability to deliver his people from oppressors and his willingness to give them second chances (and third, and fourth), even though they continually do nothing to deserve such grace. The cycles that comprise the literary structure of the book of Judges document both benefit jeopardy and revelation jeopardy. In addition to the cycles, Judges 17–21 shows how badly the situation has degenerated— even the Levites and tribal leaders were responsible for the jeopardy. (Add the violations of Eli's sons to this list as well.) These actions represent a system breakdown and eventuated in the transitional period in which the ark left the land, symbolizing Yahweh's self-imposed exile.

With the failure of priestly and tribal leadership, another form of leadership was warranted that would contribute to adherence to the law and would also reflect accurately what God's leadership was like. Thus began the phase that introduced kingship.

JEOPARDY IN THE DAVIDIC PHASE

In the Davidic phase of the covenant (kingship), initial incidents of jeopardy concerned which dynasty was going to serve the function of being the conduit of this phase of revelation. Subsequent jeopardy (David's family problems) serves to threaten the clarity of God's revelation just as the failure to drive out the Canaanites had in the previous phase. If the king, a representative of God's kingship, is abusing the power with which he is entrusted, he is not providing a very accurate picture of God's kingship. The long-term jeopardy in this phase concerns whether or not the Davidic line will retain the privileges of kingship (cf., Isa. 7:9).

Revelation Jeopardy

If human kingship is to be a vehicle by which God's kingship is revealed, the people of the kingdom must have a correct understanding of the role of the king. If inappropriate expectations of kingship exist, then God's revelation of his kingship will be in jeopardy. This can be illustrated very clearly in the teaching and ministry of Jesus. He had to recondition the Jews' ideas about the kingdom of God and the nature of the Messiah before he could reveal the role he had come to play.

As a result, when the people came to demand that Samuel find a king for them, their concept of what a king was supposed to do created immediate revelation jeopardy. They were not looking for a king who would be God's representative—they were looking for one who would be his replacement (1 Sam. 8:7–9). God chose to show them the error of this course of action by ostensibly allowing the process to go forward under their terms.[2] They thought that their problem (constant oppression) was political, therefore they concluded that they needed a king to lead them forth in battle (a political solution). In reality their problem was spiritual (benefits forfeited because of covenant violations); therefore, they needed a spiritual solution. But they had to find that out their own way.

The entire length of Saul's reign was characterized by jeopardy, primarily abortive and revelation jeopardy. The establishment of kingship was aborted because Saul never achieved the expectations of either the people or God. The rejection of Saul and his line by the Lord is the key feature in the narratives from 1 Samuel 13–15. Consequently God chose another line by which his kingship would be revealed. It is of interest to note that during a large part of Saul's reign God's kingship was being revealed, but through David, not Saul. This was especially evident in David's defeat of Goliath when David showed a clear understanding that the one leading Israel's armies was the Lord, not the king. The Spirit of the Lord left

Saul and came upon David (1 Sam. 16) and David became the channel of revelation even though he did not sit on the throne.

Once David occupied the throne, God's revelation of his kingship moved forward full throttle. The ark was brought back into prominence and the land was fully possessed. The law was obeyed and the benefits were procured. Unfortunately, David also brought about revelation jeopardy in his sin against Uriah and Bathsheba. His abuse of power (taking what he wanted and engineering murder as he pleased) was not an accurate reflection of God's kingship. This revelation jeopardy did not result in benefit jeopardy, for David had been promised unconditionally that his son would succeed him to the throne. Nonetheless, David did not enjoy peace within his family as his sons continually struggled with abuse of power.

After David's death and Solomon's accession to the throne, revelation jeopardy continued as Solomon failed in numerous respects. Added to that also at this juncture was benefit jeopardy since the succession of Solomon's son to the throne had not been vouchsafed in the covenant. Subsequently ten of the tribes were lost to future Davidic rulers.

The documents of the monarchy period (especially those of 1 and 2 Kings) communicate the revelation jeopardy in one king after another being cited for failure to depart from a predecessor's sins or to fulfill the Davidic ideal.[3] Thus, king after king brought only dishonor to God's name rather than offering a reflection of God's kingship in his rule ("walking before the LORD"). At the same time benefit jeopardy continued to be evident on the level of the people as a whole, though that is more the theme of the prophetic books than of the historical literature.

The resolution of revelation jeopardy during this period can be seen most clearly in the Elijah and Elisha narratives and the siege of Sennacherib.

The Elijah and Elisha Narratives

Ahab and Jezebel attempt to establish Baal as the national deity of Israel in place of Yahweh. This intent concerns national and even cosmic kingship. Not only does Ahab fail to reflect the kingship of Yahweh in his own rule, he goes so far as to deny kingship to Yahweh and seeks to replace him with another deity. The prophet Elijah is the champion brought forward to represent Yahweh's claims. As a result, through this period, Yahweh's kingship is revealed through Elijah, and his successor, Elisha, rather than through the apostate rebel kings of the house of Omri. God's revelation is the common denominator that defines the logic of the narrator's treatment of Elijah and Elisha.

Elijah is first introduced when he proclaims a drought on the land (1 Kings 17). In this chapter Yahweh's control over the elements that were most closely associated with Baal demonstrate that the usurper is impotent. The drought is not confined to Israel, but is in Baal's homeland of Sidon as well (1 Kings 17:9). Yet Yahweh is well able to provide selectively despite the drought. Both Elijah and the widow of Zarephath are cared for (Elijah being from Yahweh's territory and the widow being from Baal's territory).[4] The contest on Mount Carmel is a more public opportunity for Yahweh to demonstrate his superiority to Baal: that he alone is God (1 Kings 18:21, 36–39).

The other main events of Elijah's career portray him in the role of passing judgment on kings. Ahab's manipulation of the justice system to cause the death of Naboth and to procure his property, and Ahaziah's inquiry of Baal are both denounced by Elijah. The LORD's kingship brings even kings to justice.

Elisha's activities, while showing paradigmatic similarities to the career of Elijah, focus on reflecting God's kingship at different levels. Most obvious is the military success that comes through Elisha. His contribution to victory over the Aramaeans (2 Kings 6:8–23), his role in the termination of the siege of Samaria, and his involvement in the succession of Hazael to the throne in Damascus (8:7–15) and Jehu to the throne in Israel (9:1–13) over and above his prophecies of victory (3:13–20; 13:14–19) all show him as the one through whom the LORD brings victory. This is recognized in his title "the chariots and horsemen of Israel" (13:14), which had also been attributed to Elijah (2:12).[5]

Additionally, Elisha is seen providing for the needs of

individuals (e.g., 2 Kings 2:19–22; 4:1–7; 4:42–44; 6:1–7) and being concerned about justice for individuals (e.g., 8:1–6). His healing of Naaman's leprosy is not something a king would necessarily be expected to do, but in the context it avoids what could have become an international incident (5:5–7). The king never thinks of consulting the LORD about the matter, and Elisha steps in to take over in the wake of the king's inability to deal with the problem.

The prophets Elijah and Elisha both serve as the instrument through whom God's kingship is revealed, and in effect bring a resolution to the revelation jeopardy created by the unfaithfulness of the kings.[6] The prophets thus begin serving as the emissaries of God.

Hezekiah and Sennacherib

Revelation jeopardy occurs in combination with circumstantial jeopardy in the case of Hezekiah and Sennacherib. Sennacherib's siege of Jerusalem seems an insurmountable obstacle that conflicts with the LORD's promised protection of his people. His sovereignty was not only in question, but was directly challenged by the Assyrian rhetoric (2 Kings 19:10–13). Clear revelation of God's kingship could be jeopardized if Hezekiah were to fail to trust the Lord. Thus Isaiah warns him about relying on Egypt. The reality of the danger is seen from the earlier failure of Hezekiah's father, Ahaz, who relied on political alliances and thereby incurred benefit jeopardy (Isa. 7:7–17).

Fortunately Hezekiah chooses a faith response and in so doing paves the way for a miraculous deliverance from the Assyrian army (2 Kings 19:35).

Benefit Jeopardy

A few instances of benefit jeopardy have already been identified. At the division of the kingdom the Davidic house loses the benefit of kingship over the ten northern tribes. Then Ahaz is threatened with loss of the benefits of office in Isaiah 7:9 (where clear covenant terminology is used). Benefit jeopardy for David's house means that they were in danger of losing the throne.[7] But in a correlating way Israel is exposed to benefit jeopardy in that they could lose their king (or their right to have their own king). This is coupled with the benefit jeopardy related to previous phases that could eventuate in the loss of their land.

The proclamation of this benefit jeopardy became the role of the classical prophets. Their indictment oracles focused on the violation of the law and the covenant while their judgment oracles pronounced the reality of benefit jeopardy: Israel would be driven from its land, decimated as a people, and deprived of its status as an independent nation with its own king.

JEOPARDY IN THE NEW COVENANT

During the entire transitional period from the Exile through the Persian and Greek periods, Israel was living in a land that was theirs yet not theirs. They were under foreign rule. This obstacle created circumstantial jeopardy for any continuation or reactivation of the covenant benefits.

More significant jeopardy occurs during the life and ministry of Jesus. Circumstantial jeopardy is most evident when he is crucified and the faithful are left to wonder what will become of God's program with Jesus dead. Again, as always, circumstantial jeopardy is resolved through supernatural intervention. The resurrection not only resolves the jeopardy but provides the means by which relationship with God becomes available on a brand new level—and along with it comes the means for internalization of the law that the proclamation of the new covenant had mentioned.

Throughout the ministry of Jesus, and continuing after his resurrection, benefit jeopardy existed for those who refused to accept that Jesus is God's Messiah through whom salvation is provided and the kingdom of God is to be realized. As always, the benefits of any particular phase of the covenant would not be enjoyed by those who did not recognize the hand of God at work.

In all of these cases Yahweh is doing whatever must be done to vouchsafe the revelation of himself. For example, 1 Samuel 12:22, "For the sake of his great name the LORD will not reject his people, because the LORD was pleased to make you his own." God's goal is revelation. Although his program for revelation is jeopardized by an uncooperative people, he is determined that his entire revelation be accomplished. In fact, his accomplishment of it despite the people can itself become part of the revelation (Isa. 43:25; 48:9, 11; Jer. 14:7, 21; Ezek. 20:9–44; Dan. 9:17, 19; etc.).

NOTES

[1]L. Helyer, "The Separation of Abram and Lot: Its Significance in the Patriarchal Narratives" *JSOT* 26 (1983): 77–88.

[2]Lyle Eslinger, *Kingship of God in Crisis* (Sheffield: Almond, 1985), 268–69.

[3]For a detailed analysis of the various formulas used in Kings see A. F. Campbell, *Of Prophets and Kings* (Washington, D.C.: Catholic Biblical Association of America, 1986), 144–51.

[4]Leah Bronner, *The Stories of Elijah and Elisha* (Leiden: Brill, 1968), 84–85.

[5]See NIV Study Bible, 526 (note on 2 Kings 2:12).

[6] Cf. Bronner. Though Bronner emphasizes the prophets' struggle against paganism, statements throughout her book also suggest the line of logic presented above, e.g., "The story of Elisha shows once again that it is not Baal but God who rules the earth and bestows blessing on man and beast" (p.74). She further admits that issues of kingship, not paganism, underlie some of the stories (e.g., Naboth, 137–38). The polemics against paganism are the mechanism used to affirm Yahweh's kingship.

[7]See A. Gileadi, "The Davidic Covenant: A Theological Basis for Corporate Protection," in *Israel's Apostasy and Restoration*, ed. A. Gileadi (Grand Rapids: Baker, 1988), 157–63.

7

CONDITIONALITY
OF THE COVENANT

If covenant jeopardy is a major theme of the writers of Scripture, what are the implications concerning the issue of conditionality or unconditionality of the covenants? What aspect of the covenant can be truly in jeopardy? If a covenant is unconditional how can it be jeopardized? A more far-reaching question is whether conditionality is a relevant topic for discussion.

To begin, we can state without argument that Israel's enjoyment of the blessings of the covenant in any particular generation would be granted by everyone as being conditional. This is the benefit jeopardy of which we have already spoken. The covenant curses as well as the prophetic messages of the classical period firmly establish the fact that Israel's disobedience can bring about at least the temporary loss of both the land and other benefits. The controversy begins, however, when the discussion turns to the covenants themselves. Can the Abrahamic covenant be revoked? In what senses was the Abrahamic covenant in jeopardy? Did the jeopardy of the Mosaic covenant or the Davidic covenant affect only those phases or did they also represent jeopardy for the foundational Abrahamic covenant? Can Israel be replaced? These questions need to be pursued in light of the concept of the covenant having a revelatory purpose and in the understanding of covenant jeopardy as discussed in the previous chapter.

Once Abraham's line has been chosen as the instrument of revelation, there is never any suggestion of revoking that choice (even at the golden-calf incident, Moses' line would have been the sole survivors of Jacob's family). Once the law has been given there is no possibility of revoking the law or of God's revealing his character a different way. Once the Davidic line has been chosen, there is no option of God's revealing his kingship through another line instead.[1] Once the covenant phases have been viewed as having a revelatory function it is clear that the revelation proceeds on the basis of that covenant *regardless of the level of cooperation*. Once revelation has occurred, it cannot be taken back or undone.

If we once accept that the covenant represents a program of revelation, we must then ask what is the intended duration of that program? Is God's self-revelation an ongoing task that will span the entire length of human history or is there a point at which God has stated or will state that his self-revelation is complete? The revelation to which I am referring, of course, is that which has been termed special revelation. General revelation, in contrast, has always been ongoing and always will be. But God's program of special revelation was carried out by means of Israel. As I have maintained, that is what they were chosen for. There is very little that could be identified as special revelation that did not come through Israel.[2]

The New Testament evidence is unanimous in suggesting that God's program of special revelation came to a conclusion in Christ and the accompanying New Testament canon, and one would search in vain for scholars who would disagree. F. F. Bruce expresses the opinion most forthrightly in his comments on Hebrews 1:2.

> Priest and prophet, sage and singer were in their several ways His spokesmen; yet all the successive acts and varying modes of revelation in the ages before Christ came did not add up to the fullness of what God had to say. His word was not completely uttered until Christ came; but when Christ came, the word spoken in Him was indeed God's final word. In Him all the promises of God met with the answering "Yes!" which seals their fulfillment to His people and evokes

from them an answering "Amen!" The story of divine
revelation is a story of progression up to Christ, but there is
no progression beyond him. It is "at the end of these days"
that God has spoken in Him, and by this phrase our author
means much more than "recently"; it is a literal rendering of
the Hebrew phrase which is used in the Old Testament to
denote the epoch when the words of the prophets will be
fulfilled, and its use here means that the appearance of
Christ "once for all at the end of the age" has inaugurated
that time of fulfillment. God's previous spokesmen were his
servants, but for the proclamation of His last word to man
He has chosen His Son.[3]

There can be no greater revelation than Christ. Once Christ
has come there is no need for anything more to be said about
God, indeed, there is nothing more that can be said. Likewise,
the revelation through Christ is not in itself a progressive
revelation that continues growing and developing throughout
this age. It is a once-for-all revelation. What Christ did and who
Christ is has been revealed in the New Testament and is a
matter of record. Thus we may conclude that God's program of
revelation came to a close in Christ and the New Testament
canon.[4]

Logic now demands that the conclusion be drawn. If Israel
was chosen as God's instrument for special revelation, and if
that program of special revelation has been completed, then
Israel's task is done. That for which they were chosen has been
accomplished. God no longer has need of a people to carry out
a revelatory function. The covenant, as a revelatory program,
has run its course. To say that the revelatory function of Israel
has come to an end, however, is not to say that Israel as a
national entity has no further role to play. Likewise it does not
necessarily mean that the covenant promises are no longer
valid.[5] There is a difference between forfeiting on a mortgage
and paying it off. Although both of them mean no more
payments, in the latter you own the house. To carry the
analogy further, not every missed payment means that the
mortgage will be foreclosed, though such negligence will result

in penalties and create a certain amount of jeopardy to the mortgage.

But one must also recall that the covenant program of revelation was only an objective to a greater goal. In the process of revealing himself to us, God has revealed his plan of salvation so that a relationship is possible. As a result, all those, Jew or Gentile, who respond to that revelation and that means of salvation through faith become the elect people of God— elect as heirs of salvation rather than as channels of revelation. In that sense the covenant concept rolls over from being a program of revelation to providing a plan for salvation, and it defines the way that this salvation is provided. It is in this light that the issue of covenant conditionality must be reexamined.

THE CASE FOR UNCONDITIONALITY

In general, the more continuity-oriented one's system, the more one emphasizes the spiritual aspect of the blessings alone and the greater [the] tendency to see the covenants as conditional. The more discontinuity-oriented one's system, the greater the emphasis on all elements of covenant blessing and the greater the stress on the unconditional element in them.[6]

Those who contend for the unconditional nature of the Abrahamic and Davidic covenants have several reasons why they consider this to be an important issue. Some of them revolve around the status of the Jewish people today. Are they still the covenanted people of God for whom the land of Israel is reserved? Those who argue that the Abrahamic covenant is unconditional contend that God still intends the blessing of the land to be for the Jews because that covenant has never been revoked, nor could it ever be. They maintain that the church does not replace Israel, for Paul preserves a distinction between them and continues to see a future for Israel (1 Cor. 10:32; Rom. 11).

If these covenants are understood literally and uncondition- ally, then Israel has a future that is distinct from the church. On this basis dispensationalists subscribe to a literal millennium for Israel, which Messiah will establish at His Second Advent.[7]

The case for unconditionality is also made on the basis of the claim that neither the Abrahamic nor Davidic covenants list any conditions when they are ratified. They are unilateral, not bilateral, and, as such, are not subject to cancellation. Additionally the language of the covenants suggests an everlasting quality to the agreement (Gen. 13:15; 17:7–8; 2 Sam. 7:13–16; Ps. 89:28–37).

Finally, many argue for unconditionality based on their understanding of the nature of the covenant relationship.

"Land" and "house" (= dynasty), the objects of the Abrahamic and Davidic covenants respectively, are indeed the most prominent gifts of the suzerain in the Hittite and Syro-Palestinian political reality, and like the Hittite grants so also the grant of land to Abraham and the grant of "house" to David are unconditional. Thus we read in the treaty of Hattusilis III (or Tudhaliyas IV) with Ulmi-Tešup of Datasa: "After you, your son and grandson will possess it, nobody will take it away from them. If one of your descendants sins the king will prosecute him at his court. Then when he is found guilty . . . if he deserves death he will die. But nobody will take away from the descendant of Ulmi-Tešub *either his house or his land* in order to give it to a descendant of somebody else."[8]

THE CASE FOR CONDITIONALITY

Despite the language that is used in the passages cited above, other passages can be persuasively cited to indicate a conditional aspect to the Abrahamic and Davidic covenants. If a covenant is truly unconditional, then one would think it could not be broken. Yet as early as Genesis 17:14 such a possibility is mentioned. In the same vein, numerous passages in 1 Kings place explicit conditions on succession to and retention of the throne of Israel (2:2–4; 6:12; 8:25; 9:4–9). More to the point, however, is that those who make a case for conditionality do so not by suggesting that the covenant of Abraham is no longer in existence, but by maintaining that Israel has forfeited her place in the covenant and has been replaced by the church who is now heir to the spiritual promises made through the covenant.

Before a decision can be reached concerning the conditionality or unconditionality of the covenant, the specific aspects of conditionality and unconditionality in each covenant phase must be surveyed.

CONDITIONALITY AND UNCONDITIONALITY IN THE COVENANT PHASES

In each phase of the covenant there is an emphasis on the necessity for obedience. In different phases disobedience represents different types of jeopardy. Each case must be examined carefully because jeopardy is not necessarily indicative of conditionality. Also, in each phase there is an element that is identified as a hinge point for that phase; a response that would serve as a sign of conformity to the relationship of the elect party to God, the covenant maker.[9] The hinge could be either an individual act by which one joins the community of the elect, or specific conduct (as opposed to general obedience) by which one indicates a continuing commitment to the covenant relationship. In the following analysis we will investigate (1) the expectation or necessity for obedience of the elect, and (2) the response that serves as a sign of participation in the covenant. The purpose of this section is to consider how each of these elements affects covenant conditionality.

The Abrahamic Phase
Necessity for Obedience

Before Abraham can enter into a covenant relationship, there are requests made of him. He is asked to leave his home, family, and inheritance for those that God will provide (Gen. 12:1). This, of course, places conditions only on the initiation of the covenant. Nevertheless, other passages convey that it is an expectation, if not a condition, that Abraham and his line will be characterized by a particular sort of conduct (e.g., Gen. 18:16)[10] and the continuity that exists with the Mosaic phase might go so far as to suggest that the law offered clarification of that expectation and established it as a condition.[11]

Sign of Participation: Circumcision

Circumcision is established by God as the sign of the covenant. The act of circumcision is identified by God as the way that Abraham's family will "keep" the covenant (*šamar* Gen. 17:9-10). This covenant "in their flesh" is to be an "everlasting" covenant. Those who do not do it will be cut off and the covenant considered broken (17:13-14). In this sense circumcision becomes a condition by means of which any individual Israelite would be considered to be part of the elect. It is not a condition placed on election, nor does it jeopardize the covenant program as a whole; only the individual's participation is affected.

The Mosaic Phase

Necessity for Obedience

The condition of obedience is clearest during the Mosaic phase. No one denies the conditional nature of the covenant that is set forth explicitly in the blessings and curses that accompany the ratification of the covenant (Deut. 27-28). Furthermore, the warnings of the prophets and the historical testimony confirm that the conditions were proclaimed, uncontested, and enforced.

Sign of Participation: The Sabbath

While the individual's sign of participation in the covenant is circumcision, the sign of corporate Israel's participation in the covenant is identified as the keeping of the Sabbath (Ex. 31:13-17) and their failure to do this is cited as one of the primary reasons for God's judgment of them (Ezek. 20:10-26).[12] Like circumcision, the keeping of the Sabbath is a continuous obligation required of each generation. Unlike circumcision, it is not a one-time act, but an attitude to be consistently maintained and periodically expressed in action.

The Davidic Phase

Necessity for Obedience

The fact that there are no conditions mentioned in the original proclamation of the Davidic covenant in 2 Samuel 7 does not necessarily mean that it is an unconditional covenant. David is promised unconditionally that his son will succeed him to the throne, but for the succession after Solomon, Scripture makes it eminently clear that there is a condition of obedience attached (1 Kings 2:2–4; 6:12; 8:25; 9:4–9; Ps. 132:11–12). This must be reconciled with the passages that seem to admit no possibility of forfeiture (Ps. 89:28–37; Jer. 33:19–26). One of the key issues to be decided is whether succession to the throne is a benefit of the covenant or the essence of the covenant. If it is a benefit, then it can be withheld even though the covenant itself continues to be maintained. But, if succession to the throne is simply a benefit, how can one describe the essence of the covenant?

When the Davidic covenant is established there is a differentiation made between the basis on which the covenant is made and the obedience that is expected within it. The Lord says that he will punish disobedience, but he will by no means remove his ḥesed from David's line. Therefore, even though David's line may fail to the point of not having a representative on the throne, Yahweh's ḥesed (covenant loyalty) will not be granted to another line. So, as God's program of revelation was previously bound inextricably to the people of Israel, here it is bound to the line of David. It is the essence of the covenant. Saul's ineffectiveness as a representative of God's kingship disqualified him and his line. David's effectiveness in that role was instrumental in the election of his line to fulfill the revelatory function. David had fulfilled the conditions of faithfulness and obedience before the covenant was made with him (1 Kings 3:6; 15:4–5). His descendants would have the benefits of the covenant conditioned on their obedience.[13]

Sign of Participation: Anointing

Studies of the practice of anointing in Israel have identified both "sacral" and "secular" aspects.[14] The former involves cases where God's representative does the anointing and it is viewed as establishing a vassal relationship between God and king. The secular aspect is illustrated by the examples of when people anoint the king, in which cases there is a relationship of subordinating the people to the king.[15] It is the sacral aspect that is of most significance to our discussion. Mettinger has identified the rite as a sign of election:

> The anointing amounts to a visible sign of the divine *election* of the king. Election terminology is of considerable importance in the passage. The anointing seals the divine election of David.[16]

Of additional importance Mettinger identifies a close relationship between anointing and the endowment of the Spirit of the Lord.

> The charisma is closely related to the rite itself. There are no immediate spectacular manifestations of it. From the point of view of this tradition the question of how one could know that David had the Spirit could only be answered: because he was anointed.[17]

Finally, Mettinger also concludes that the anointing with oil was a rite used upon entering into a contractual relationship.[18]

> When the stronger party anoints the weaker, we are faced with a *promissory* type of contractual relation. Thus in the nuptial anointing, where the party responsible for the anointing thereby assumes obligation. The stronger party does not thereby make himself a vassal of the weaker but assumes obligation towards the bride. When the weaker party is responsible for the unction we can speak of an *obligatory* type of contractual relations in which the vassal has to oblige himself. Thus in Idrimi and in the Assyrian Ritual the weaker party offers unction as a token of submission.[19]

One key difference in this sign of participation is that God is the one who anoints, whereas, in the other phases it was the elect who performed the sign. Also, anointing is connected more closely to the election of the king by Yahweh than to the covenant itself. In the case of David, his anointing represents his election to kingship. The covenant represents the election of his dynasty. From that point on, election to kingship also brings one into the covenant relationship.

Unlike circumcision and the keeping of the Sabbath, then, this is a sign of election rather than a sign of the covenant. I contend, however, that it is serving a function similar to the signs of the other covenants. Each of the covenant phases contains a means by which the elect demonstrate their participation in that phase. This is to be differentiated from the actual stipulations that comprise the covenant agreement itself. The act of circumcision shows an acknowledgment of God as the source of the family. The observance of the Sabbaths shows an acknowledgment of God as the source of holiness (Ezek. 20:12). The anointing ceremony as initiated by God shows a recognition of the king's subordination to divine kingship with Yahweh being the source of kingship. This is not something that carries any sense of conditionality. It is promissory in the sense that it is an extension of the *hesed* of Yahweh to the king.

The New Covenant Phase
Necessity for Obedience

From the initial proclamation of the new covenant phase it was clear that the law would still be important (it would be in their hearts) and that obedience to the law would be expected. When the new covenant is implemented in the teachings of Christ, obedience is still very much an emphasis. Christ's admonitions to his disciples (John 14:15–15:17), Peter's descriptions of believers (1 Peter 1:2) and Paul's advice to the churches (Rom. 16:25–26) consistently demonstrate that obedience is expected of those who are the elect of the new covenant.

Sign(s) of Participation

There are a number of elements identified as signs of the new covenant. Perhaps the one with most textual claim is communion ("This cup is the new covenant in my blood, which is poured out for you" [Luke 22:20]). The periodic observance of communion is similar to the periodic observance of the Sabbath in the Mosaic phase.

Secondly, the combination of repentance and baptism is a sign of the elect's participation in the new covenant (Acts 2:38). Baptism is an initiation sign just as circumcision was for the Abrahamic phase. It accompanies the endowment of the Spirit just as did anointing in the Davidic phase. These signs demonstrate an acknowledgment of God as the source of our salvation.

Conclusions

Does the Expectation of Obedience
Make a Covenant Conditional?

In each of the phases of the covenant the expectation of obedience is connected either to the initiation of the covenant or to the benefits of the covenant. If one were to view the enjoyment of the benefits or the delivery of the benefits as the essence of the covenant, then benefit jeopardy would mean that the covenant itself was threatened. But in the model under consideration here—with revelation as the essence of the covenant—the jeopardy to benefits only affects the uncooperative elect, it does nothing to damage God's revelatory program. For instance, in the Mosaic phase, while obedience to the law is certainly expected and enjoyment of the benefits is conditioned on that obedience, I contend that the very essence of the law is not the socioreligious system that it articulates, but the God that it reveals. Given this revelatory function of the law, the Mosaic covenant in which the law is contained can be seen as unconditional. The revelation of God through the covenant, law, is an accomplished fact. His holiness is illustrated in the law—even in those sections which represent an obsolete socioreligious system.[20] Thus, I conclude that the expectation of obedience makes the enjoyment of the benefits of the covenant conditional, but does not make the covenant itself conditional.

*Does the Existence of a Sign of Participation
Make the Covenant Conditional?*

If one were to view participation in the covenant as a privilege that could be extended to others should the initial elect renege, then the existence of the sign could represent a degree of conditionality. But I submit that nothing in the Old Testament gives any indication that any other party could potentially serve as God's revelatory elect in any of the phases. The only sense in which Israel's position as the elect of Yahweh could be jeopardized would be in the covenant roll over from revelatory election to soteric election. This will be addressed in the next chapter in the discussion concerning the people of God. The signs concern any given individual's inclusion among the elect and concern the benefits that the elect enjoy, but have no effect on which corporate group is the elect.

NOTES

[1]The statements made to Jeroboam in 1 Kings 11:34–39 suggest that Jeroboam may be able to share in the function of the covenant and enjoy benefits similar to those of the house of David, but not to the exclusion of David's line or as a replacement of David's line.

[2]Special revelation is comprised primarily of Scripture. The acts of God in history are certainly revelatory, but if they are not interpreted by verbal or written communication, they only constitute general revelation. The oracles of the prophets would have had to have been considered special revelation even before they were inscripturated and the same is true of the teachings and deeds of Christ. All of these are recorded for us only in the pages of the Bible; thus, while special revelation came through different channels, the Bible remains our only source of special revelation. While most of the channels of special revelation were associated with Israel, there are isolated exceptions. Balaam is one, and Luke, thought by many to be a Gentile, another.

[3]F. F. Bruce, *The Epistle to the Hebrews* (Grand Rapids: Eerdmans, 1964), 3. Likewise, Leon Morris speaks of Christ as the "consummation of the revelatory process" in "Hebrews" in *Expositor's Bible Commentary*, vol. 12, ed. F. Gaebelein (Grand Rapids: Zondervan, 1981), 13.

[4]It should be noted, however, that there are some who believe that Israel still has a revelatory service to perform in the future; see Robert Saucy, "Israel and the Church: A Case for Discontinuity" in *Continuity and Discontinuity*, ed. John S. Feinberg (Wheaton: Crossway, 1988), 256–57. The Council on Biblical Inerrancy denies "that any normative revelation has been given since the completion of the New Testament writings" (Article V of the Chicago

statement). I am not willing to contend that there cannot possibly have been any further special revelation after the New Testament period. For instance, what of the role of the two witnesses in Revelation? For a thourough defense of the idea that Israel still will have a future revelatory role, see R. L. Saucy, *The Case for Progressive Dispensationalism* (Grand Rapids: Zondervan, 1993), 317–19. Nevertheless, I still maintain that God's *program* of special revelation is complete.

[5]I was amazed when late in my research I encountered the following statement, which so closely echoed some of the elements that I am proposing. "Because of that choice [Abraham and his seed] the Jewish nation became the exclusive channel through which God chose to reveal himself to the world. But now that the Messiah has come and God's revelation to mankind has been completed, written in a book and made available to the people of all nations with nothing more to be added, there is no further need for a separate people or nation to serve that purpose"(Lorraine Boettner, *The Meaning of the Millennium*, ed. R. G. Clouse [Downers Grove: InterVarsity Press, 1977], 52–53). However, the similarity stops there as Boettner goes on to say that once the Messiah fulfills his role, Israel's role is likewise complete. "All of those elements belonged to the kindergarten stage of redemption, and on completion of that atonement at Calvary, all of those things [i.e., the things that set Israel apart] passed away as a unit." (Ibid.) It is clear that he is still operating within a system that is seen to cohere through the concept of redemption.

[6]John S. Feinberg, "Systems of Discontinuity" in *Continuity and Discontinuity*, 80.

[7]Paul Enns, *The Moody Handbook of Theology* (Chicago: Moody Press, 1989), 523.

[8]M. Weinfeld, "The Covenant of Grant in the Old Testament and in the Ancient Near East" *JAOS* 90 (1970): 189.

[9]See R. T. Beckwith's helpful chart in his article, "The Unity and Diversity of God's Covenants" *TB* 38 (1987): 105.

[10]For a fuller treatment see B. K. Waltke, "The Phenomenon of Conditionality Within Unconditional Covenants" in *Israel's Apostasy and Restoration*, ed. A. Gileadi (Grand Rapids: Baker, 1988), 128–30; Daniel P. Fuller, *Gospel and Law: Contrast or Continuum?* (Grand Rapids: Eerdmans, 1980), 134–45; and Ronald Youngblood, "The Abrahamic Covenant: Conditional or Unconditional?" in *The Living and Active Word of God* (Winona Lake: Eisenbrauns, 1983), 36–41.

[11]For a position that draws together the Abrahamic and Sinai covenants, see W. J. Dumbrell, "The Prospect of Unconditionality in the Sinaitic Covenant" in *Israel's Apostasy and Restoration*, 141–54.

[12]*TDOT* I:181–83.

[13]G. E. Gerbrandt, *Kingship According to the Deuteronomistic History* (Atlanta: Scholars Press, 1986), 167.

[14]T. N. D. Mettinger, *King and Messiah* (Lund: Gleerup, 1976), 185–232.

[15]Ibid. Mettinger, not only traces the development of these concepts in the history of interpretation (185–88), but also offers a full lexical and syntactical

analysis of the distribution of both noun and verb (188–94). He also presents his theory that there is a developing "sacralization" of the rite, but this theory is based on source-critical conclusions that I find unconvincing.

[16]Ibid., 207.

[17]Ibid.

[18]Ibid., 211–22. In this connection, Mettinger views anointing as a rite of ratification.

[19]Ibid., 222.

[20]This is not to suggest that the law is without moral imperatives. See discussion in chapter 10.

8

ASKING THE RIGHT QUESTIONS

WHAT WAS IN JEOPARDY?

Why has conditionality been such a controversial and difficult issue? The problem has been caused at least in part by the fact that in most views regarding the covenant the purpose or essence of the covenant has been identified with one or more of the major benefits to the elect of the covenant. When this is the case, total covenant jeopardy (dissolution and forfeiture) is difficult to isolate from benefit jeopardy (which is present nearly everywhere).

For instance, if promise is the purpose of the covenant, and the promises are conditional, how can the covenant not be conditional? If relationship, or the establishment of a relationship (salvation), is the objective of the covenant, yet relationship can be jeopardized by disobedience, then the covenant itself is vulnerable to dissolution.

In contrast, the proposal under consideration in this book (see chapter 2) sees the central purpose of the covenant as something distinct from the benefits promised to the elect party. As a result, benefit jeopardy has no impact on the purpose of the covenant. Furthermore, there is no other true jeopardy to the covenant. Circumstantial jeopardy as well as revelation jeopardy are perceptions only. God's sovereignty overcomes them. Abortive jeopardy is only present in the initiating phase. All of the conditions are attached to the benefits and it is only the benefits that are ever in jeopardy. Thus, the covenant itself, understood as a program of revelation, is part of the immutable plan of God, and can never be in true jeopardy.

But all of this does not answer the questions concerning the status of Israel today. If the covenant could not be put in jeopardy and there was nothing that Israel or anyone else could do to hinder the covenant's accomplishing its purpose, do we conclude that Israel continues to serve as the instrument of God's revelatory program? Or to phrase it another way: Is ethnic Israel still to be considered the people of God?

This is a rephrasing of some of the initial questions. Instead of asking whether the covenant is conditional, we have now asked: Is God's program of revelation conditional? Did God ever choose any other people to carry out his program of revelation? This was answered in the negative. However, if the covenant is defined as a revelatory program, it has a limited term of service, as discussed in the previous chapter. Once the revelatory task is complete, can God dismiss the people he has used to accomplish it? Are the benefits of the covenant still available even though the program has been completed? To address this we must consider how we understand the concept, "people of God."

PEOPLE OF GOD

In the Mosaic phase the key point of election is that Israel is chosen to be the *people of God*. I have defined and interpreted this phrase in a revelatory sense. With the new covenant, the new elect body is identified as all who respond in faith to the salvation offered through Christ. This is a soteriological definition. The logical result of this is the conclusion that the concept, people of God, has been redefined in the New Testament. As N. Thomas Wright states it, "Paul is consistently undermining the traditional Jewish view of election, and establishing a new view of the people of God."[1]

In this section the following sequence of propositions will be addressed: (1) The people of God has been redefined soteriologically; (2) in this new definition, Gentiles can now be part of the people of God; (3) ethnic Israel is no longer the people of God in the original sense, but (4) is welcome to be part of the new soteric people of God; and (5) there is reason to expect that Israel will ultimately accept that invitation.

People of God Soteriologically Defined

The clearest New Testament support for this proposition is in Galatians 3. After introducing Abraham as an example of righteousness gained by faith, verse seven asserts that "those who believe are children of Abraham." Wright sees this redefinition as offering an explanation of Paul's use of Habakkuk 2:4.

> Paul thus ties in Habakkuk's redefinition of the covenant community with the original promise to Abraham, and thereby argues that ([Gal. 3:]11a) "no-one is reckoned within the covenant community on the basis of Torah." This use of Habakkuk, it then appears, is neither as odd nor as arbitrary as it is sometimes made out to be. . . . Paul's point, in using Habakkuk in this way, is that *when* that redefinition comes about, the demarcating characteristic of the covenant people is to be precisely their *faith*, their belief in Israel's God.[2]

Verses 26–29 carry this same identification of faith as the demarcating factor of Abraham's seed:

> 26You are all sons of God through faith in Christ Jesus, 27for all of you who were baptized into Christ have clothed yourselves with Christ. 28There is neither Jew nor Greek, slave nor free, male nor female, for you are all one in Christ Jesus. 29If you belong to Christ, then you are Abraham's seed, and heirs according to the promise.

Although Galatians 3 does not use the term people of God, it imposes a soteric definition on Abraham's seed. This is also the case in Galatians 6:16 where the term *Israel of God* is used. That this definition is also applied to the people of God can be seen in Titus 2:14 where it is asserted that Christ "gave himself for us to redeem us from all wickedness and to purify for himself a people that are his very own, eager to do what is good."

Wright also sees this issue woven through Romans.

> Paul's innovation in the light of the cross and resurrection is
> that he argues from the covenant passages themselves
> (Genesis 15 and 17) that this people of God must be
> (1) worldwide and therefore (2) characterized by Christ-
> shaped faith, not by race, circumcision or Torah.[3]

Gentiles Included in the People of God

That the Gentiles were eligible for membership in the
people of God is discussed and officially confirmed at the
Jerusalem council (Acts 15:14). It is likewise articulated clearly
by both Peter and Paul.

> [19]Consequently, you are no longer foreigners and aliens,
> but fellow citizens with God's people and members of God's
> household, [20]built on the foundation of the apostles and
> prophets, with Christ Jesus himself as the chief cornerstone.
> [21]In him the whole building is joined together and rises to
> become a holy temple in the Lord. [22]And in him you too are
> being built together to become a dwelling in which God lives
> by his Spirit. (Ephesians 2:19–22)

> [9]But you are a chosen people, a royal priesthood, a holy
> nation, a people belonging to God, that you may declare the
> praises of him who called you out of darkness into his
> wonderful light. [10]Once you were not a people, but now you
> are the people of God; once you had not received mercy, but
> now you have received mercy. (1 Peter 2:9–10)

This is not a case of the Gentiles' (or the church's) taking on the
role of Israel or replacing Israel. Rather a new group is taking
shape and, though it uses the same label to indicate a special
relationship with God that Israel had, the relationship is on
quite a different basis. Therefore this is not one people
replacing another, it is one definition of people of God
replacing another. In the new definition the category then
becomes open to those to whom it had not previously been
open.[4] This exchange takes place through a multistep process.
Paul makes a case in Galatians 3 and elsewhere that Christ is
the representative of corporate Israel. We might go so far as to

say that Christ has replaced Israel in the revelatory program, at
least in the sense that he is the fulfillment of the promises and
the channel of revelation. Then the people of God become
defined as those who are "in Christ."[5]

Ethnic Israel's "People of God" Status
No Longer Relevant

With the new definition coming into existence, the old
definition is no longer sufficient or necessary. This is one of the
ways in which I understand Paul when he says that "Neither
circumcision nor uncircumcision means anything; what counts
is a new creation" (Gal. 6:15). As long as the revelatory
program existed, circumcision was the sign by which the elect
of that program were designated. But once the soteric program
commenced (and there is some overlap) the sign of participation changed (Col. 2:11–12). This is certainly reflected in the
confusion over the issue of circumcision in the early church.
Gentiles were not required to be circumcised because they were
not becoming part of the revelatory elect. Likewise the circumcision of the Jews accomplished nothing in terms of their
membership in the soteric elect, though their circumcision still
had importance for their membership in the revelatory elect.
We have discussed in previous chapters how the revelatory
function of Israel has been completed. It is therefore logical to
conclude that they can no longer be considered the people of
God by that old definition. Again Wright agrees and sees this as
a consistent affirmation in Paul's writings.

> Paul has made it clear beyond any doubt, and completely in
> line with Galatians, 1 Thessalonians 2, 2 Corinthians 3,
> Philippians 3, and the whole of Romans 1–8, that there is no
> covenant membership for Israel on the basis of racial or
> "fleshly" identity. She cannot be the people of God simply
> by clinging to ancestral privilege; that privilege reached its
> intended goal in her being the place where sin became
> concrete and concentrated.[6]

Israel Is Welcome to Be Part
of Newly Defined People of God

Nevertheless, we cannot conclude that Israel has been rejected from being considered the people of God. It is just that in order to be part of that group, as it has been redefined, Israel must conform to the new definition. The people of God are now defined soteriologically, so any Israelite who wants to be a continuing part of the people of God must respond in faith to God's provision of salvation through Christ. Paul makes all of this eminently clear in Romans 11. Early in the chapter he asserts that "God did not reject his people" (v. 2) and that they have not stumbled beyond recovery (v. 11). Finally, using the agricultural illustration of grafting, he contends that "if they do not persist in unbelief, they will be grafted in, for God is able to graft them in again" (v. 23).

> On the basis of the biblical description of "Israel" as "people of God" involving a national identity and the church as similarly "people of God" but formed from all nations, we have sought to show that these entities are not totally continuous. Rather, the Scriptures indicate that both have a place in God's plan of salvation.[7]

Israel's Ultimate Acceptance

As has long been recognized, the New Testament key to this discussion is to be found in Romans 11:25–27.

> 25I do not want you to be ignorant of this mystery, brothers, so that you may not be conceited: Israel has experienced a hardening in part until the full number of the Gentiles has come in. 26And so all Israel will be saved, as it is written:

> > "The deliverer will come from Zion;
> >   he will turn godlessness away from Jacob.
> > 27And this is my covenant with them
> >   when I take away their sins."

This passage has been interpreted many different ways and at times has been thought to be contradictory to Romans 9–10.

It is usually held that, in Romans 11, Paul predicts a large-scale entry of Jews into the Kingdom in fulfillment of the ancestral promise, after the Gentiles have been saved. There are, of course, numerous variations on this theme. Some see this sudden event as happening immediately before the Parousia, while others see it as concurrent. Some see it as involving actual conversion to Christ, while for others it is a salvation which takes place apart from Christ. Some see it as involving all Jews living at the time, others as including a large number but not all. Whatever the variation, this basic view always seems to fit very badly with Romans 9–10, where, following Galatians and Romans 1–8, Paul makes it abundantly clear that there is no covenant membership, and consequently no salvation, for those who simply rest on their ancestral privilege.[8]

Wright considers the reference to Israel in verse twenty-six a redefinition, identifying the Israel of the prophecy as God's newly defined elect, believers of all nations. He then translates, "That is how God is saving 'all Israel.'"[9] Wright's main argument is with those who contend that the ultimate salvation of Israel is taking place independent of the new definition of the people of God, i.e., that their salvation is still on the basis of ancestral privilege. While I agree with his rejecting that view, there is still the option of interpreting the passage as an expectation that there will be a massive acceptance of the new terms of the covenant and the new definition of the people of God by the Jews. This is expressed in the analysis of Hans LaRondelle.

> It is God's intention to bring natural Israel back to Himself by means of the Church of Christ. This way of saving many Jews from ethnic Israel for Christ is part of the marvelous "mystery" of God.[10]

I have no doubt that Paul has promoted a redefinition of the people of God, but I am less convinced that he has redirected the eschatological promises made to Israel, to the newly-elect, by a reinterpretation of the prophecies. Consistency suggests that Romans 9–11 must be understood as promulgating the eventual response of ethnic Israel.[11] On the one hand, there is no reason to reject the idea that there are some senses in which the newly elect become heirs to a spiritualized version of some of the promises. But on the other hand the logic of the theory I am proposing suggests that ethnic Israel may still claim the benefits of their covenant. We will return to this, but first, a summary of conclusions so far.

HAS GOD REJECTED ISRAEL?

As we have found, it is important to be clear about what is meant by this. Ethnic Israel is no longer the people of God on the basis of their ancestry alone. They were not rejected from their former status because of their unfaithfulness. Instead, that status came to an end because the revelatory function had been accomplished. The sense in which Israel can be said to have been rejected is that their refusal to accept the work of Christ on their behalf has left them outside of the people of God; not because they were kicked out, but because they refused to renew their membership in the revised program. They have not, however, been totally rejected as people of God because they can still be the people of God on the basis of faith. Any belief in a future physical, earthly kingdom of Christ must not be established on any continuing privilege of Israel's being people of God according to their prior status, but on an understanding of the elements of a former agreement that may have continuing viability. Bruce Waltke is representative of those who are not willing to see any such kingdom.

> Not one clear NT passage mentions the restoration of Israel as a political nation or predicts an earthly reign of Christ before his final appearing. None depicts the consummate glory of Christ as an earthly king ruling over the restored nation of Israel. The Spirit's silence is deafening.[12]

And again,

> As the obverse side of the NT coin bears the hard imprint that no clear passage teaches the restoration of the national Israel, its reverse side is imprinted with the hard fact that national Israel and its law have been permanently replaced by the church and the New Covenant. Without wresting

Matthew 15:13 and Mark 12:1-9, our Lord announced in these passages that the Jewish *nation* no longer has a place as the special people of God; that place has been taken by the Christian community which fulfills God's purpose for Israel.[13]

There is a difference, however, in seeing a physical earthly kingdom as a kingdom of Israel (against which Waltke objects) and a kingdom of God (for the people of God redefined). The kingdom of God is for all his people of faith. This does not prevent it from having a physical manifestation, though whatever physical aspects it has should be seen as subordinate to its spiritual aspects. That the remnant of ethnic Israel who have accepted the faith definition of the people of God should be able to enjoy that kingdom, and along with it the benefits that have been the legacy of the role they played in the revelatory plan of God is very much in line with both Old and New Testament teaching. In this sense I speak of Israel's being restored to the kingdom rather than the kingdom's being restored to Israel. But there is no reason to think that the spiritual priority of the kingdom rules out a physical reality.[14]

But what of those New Testament passages that appear to affirm the rejection of Israel, i.e., Matthew 8:12 and 21:43? These can readily be seen to apply to the unbelieving or unproductive members of Israel. As D. A. Carson points out, Christ's words suggest a shift in the membership of God's people.

> But these verses affirm, in a way that could only shock Jesus' hearers, that the locus of the people of God would not always be the Jewish race.[15]
>
> Up to this time the Jewish religious leaders were the principal means by which God exercised his reign over his people. But the leaders failed so badly in handling God's "vineyard" and rejecting God's Son that God gave the responsibility to another people who would produce the kingdom's fruit. . . . Strictly speaking, then, v. 43 does not speak of transferring the locus of the people of God from Jews to Gentiles, though it may hint at this insofar as that locus now extends far beyond the authority of the Jewish

rulers . . . ; instead it speaks of the ending of the role the
Jewish religious leaders played in mediating God's authority.[16]

CAN GOD REJECT ISRAEL?

The fact is, God's revelation has been accomplished
through Israel. The law has been given; their history is public
record; Christ has come; salvation has been made available.
These things cannot be undone. It makes no sense then to
speak of Israel's being rejected as God's people when their
function as God's people has been completed. The concept of
God's people has been redefined. Israel was God's people in a
revelatory sense—they can never be rejected from that role
because the work is completed. Currently, God's people are
defined soteriologically, and Israel has as much an opportunity
as anyone else to be included in that designation. This
perspective suggests that the issue of conditionality is irrelevant. Israel served its years of employment, though not always
well. As a result, it did not always receive its full wages.
Nonetheless, the service was rendered, and it would be rather
shabby to revoke the pension plan. Certain privileges will
always be potentially Israel's (if conditions are met) based on
the claims of past service. Someone who has retired cannot be
fired.

AN EVERLASTING COVENANT?

If the role of Israel as the revelatory people of God has
come to an end, what should be made of all the passages that
speak of the covenant as everlasting? The phrase *berit 'olam*
occurs sixteen times in the Old Testament. It describes the
covenant with Noah (Gen. 9:16; cf. possibly Isa. 24:5), the
promise of the land to Abraham (Ps. 105:10; 1 Chron. 16:17),
the Davidic covenant (2 Sam. 23:5; Isa. 55:3), and the new
covenant (Isa. 61:8; Jer. 32:40; 50:5; Ezek. 16:60; 37:26), and is
used in connection with the various signs of the covenants
(circumcision, Gen. 17:7, 13, 19; Sabbath, Ex. 31:16; shewbread,
Lev. 24:8).

The Hebrew term *'olam* has been somewhat controversial,

but a general consensus has developed in recent years that is important for our discussion. Though typically translated "forever" or "everlasting" *'olam* is now understood as a term that is less philosophically abstract.[17] Possible translations include "indefinitely, permanently, in perpetuity or perpetual, enduring, always." It expresses open-endedness or an agreement without specified end. Key passages that show this more restricted meaning are 1 Samuel 1:22 and Jeremiah 17:4 (see also 1 Sam. 2:30 and Deut. 15:17).

What should be understood, then, when the text speaks of a *berit 'olam?* The implication of the terminology is that these agreements are not temporary, not stopgap, nor on a trial basis. They are permanent in the sense that no other alternative arrangement to serve that purpose is envisioned. This is even implied in the foundational wording of the covenant with Israel. It has been recognized that the affirmation "I will be your God" implies "I (alone) will be your God."[18] This suggests that the second part of the phrase, "You will be my people" should likewise be understood to imply "You (alone) shall be my people." That does not mean that the purpose it serves will never be obsolete. Circumcision became obsolete even though it was described as a *berit 'olam.* So Wright observes, "The Torah is given for a specific period of time, and is then set aside—not because it was a bad thing now happily abolished, but because it was a good thing whose purpose has now been accomplished."[19] Such agreements therefore are specified as commitment to a particular course of action that rules out opting for other alternatives in the future.

Even though this more restricted understanding of *'olam* reduces our expectations of what the description conveys, there are also two senses in which the covenant transcends the revelatory role of Israel that it brought into reality. The first is that since the covenant is fulfilled in Christ, the aspects that he fulfilled retain their validity (e.g., the Davidic monarchy, the fulfillment of the law): thus, aligning with passages such as Jeremiah 31:35–37 and 33:24–26. The second sense in which the covenant continues on is that Israel's election can be transferred from their revelatory role into the redefined people of God.

Therefore they have not had the possibility of that status removed from them.

DOES ISRAEL HAVE AN INDEPENDENT ROLE?

Traditional dispensationalism has maintained that there are now two distinct peoples of God: Israel as the earthly people of God and the church as the heavenly people of God.[20] In contrast modern dispensationalism maintains a more nuanced stance.

> Israel and the church are in one sense *a united people* of God (they participate in the same new covenant), while in another sense they remain separate in their identity and so comprise *differing peoples* of God. (Israel is given territorial and political aspects of the new-covenant promise not applicable to the church.) Israel and the church are in fact one people of God, who together share in the forgiveness of sins through Christ and partake of his indwelling Spirit with its power for covenant faithfulness, while they are nonetheless distinguishable covenant participants comprising what is one unified people.[21]

This is not far removed from the position adopted here, though I believe that there are ways of maintaining a distinct identity for Israel without retaining the people-of-God label. The text of the New Testament offers no substantiation for identifying ethnic Israel as an independent people of God. Those who believe are part of the worldwide soteric people of God, which is the only people of God in existence. Nevertheless, Israel still could be recognized as an identifiable subset within the people of God in that they are still heirs to certain promises made to them in their revelatory function. I do not see those promises as having been transferred. Those benefits were the result of the role Israel played and the church has not taken over that role. If the church has not taken over that role, then there is no reason for the church to inherit those benefits. Perhaps an illustration will help clarify the difference.

A restaurant made an agreement with the homeowner who lived next door. The agreement stipulated that the restaurant be allowed to construct its sign on the homeowner's property. In return there would be no charge to the homeowner's family when they ate at the restaurant. There was only one condition: The homeowner would not allow his property to be used for advertisement for the restaurant across the street. Once construction of the sign began, the competitor, seeing an opportunity, offered significant compensation for the family to post its advertisement. Lured by the potential profits, the homeowner also allowed the competition to advertise on his property. As might be expected, this incident led to the original restaurant's revoking the family's privileges until the competitor's offending advertising was taken down. Finally the neighboring restaurant's sign was completed, the homeowner complied with the original agreement, and all was well. Shortly thereafter, another incident developed in which the homeowner put up a billboard for the competition (they just could not resist the monetary gain). Would the original restaurant now have any right to issue a letter stating that the family no longer had the expressed privileges? Certainly the withholding of privileges could be understood as long as the competing billboard was being displayed. But the fact remains that the first restaurant's sign remains on the neighbor's property. Would there, then, be any point in choosing another family to which to extend the privilege of eating for free at the restaurant? NO! The privilege of free food is not key; the sign is the key factor. It is permanently affixed and therefore the privileges should always be available at any time, and for as long as, the conditions are met—not just during the time of construction.

EXCURSUS: AFTERMATH ORACLES

Illustrations and analogies aside, is there scriptural evidence that suggests that ethnic Israel retains the options of the benefits from their revelatory role? As Waltke observed, the New Testament is lacking such clear evidence, but that could simply be a reflection of the fact that its interest is in the redefined people of God and in soteriological matters. We have all grown used to the fact that the selectivity of the biblical authors has consigned some topics to obscurity. Arguments from silence only gain strength when it can be established that

	Subjects Addressed in Aftermath Oracles TOTAL # Oracles = 122	ASSYRIAN PERIOD				BABYLONIAN PERIOD			POST-EXILIC PERIOD				
		Amo	Hos	Isa	Mica	Zeph	Jer	Ezk	Hag	Joel	Obd	Zech	
		2	7	28	3	5	28	14	2	4	1	28	
Covenant	Regathered; Possess Land	1	2	5	1	1	18	10				2	40
	Re-elect; Holy		3	3			5	2				4	17
	Davidic King	1	1	1			3	2	1			2	11
	Multiply People			1	1		4	3					9
	Covenant Made			1	1		3	3					8
Political	Delivered by YHWH			5		1	5	2	1			4	18
	Protected by YHWH			3			2	1	1			5	12
	Defeat/Judgment Nations			4		1	4	2	1	1		5	18
	Security			5	1	1	5	3				2	17
	Peace	1		4	1					1		1	8
	Nations Coming			7			1	1				4	13
	Reunited		1				3	1					5
	YHWH Reigns			1	1		1				1	1	5
	New Leaders			1			1						2
	Pre-eminence			2	3							2	7
	Possess Enemies	1					1				1		3
	Rely on YHWH			1	1								2
	Law from Zion			1	1								2
	Jerusalem Rebuilt			1			4	2					7
	Jerusalem Glorified			2				1				1	4
Spiritual	Sin Removed/Forgiven		1	2			3	3	1			2	12
	Ashamed of Sin		2				1	3				1	7
	YHWH in Midst			1			1		1			3	6
	Spirit Within							4				1	5
	Purge of Wicked			1		1		4				2	8
	Faithful to YHWH		1		1								2
	Fear/Serve/Worship YHWH			1			4	1				1	7
	Know YHWH			2				1		1		1	5
	Seek YHWH						1					1	2
	Reproach Removed		2			1							3
	Keep Law						1	2					3
	Temple								1			2	3
Socio-Econ.	Prosperity/Fertility	1	1	4			3	4	1			4	18
	Justice/Righteousness		1	3			3						7
Misc.	Cosmic Effects									2		1	3
	Nations Brought Against Jerusalem											1	1

there was both opportunity and inherent obligation that an issue be addressed. Waltke's arguments then, though well-taken, do not offer closure to the issue in its entirety. That ethnic Israel is no longer identifiable as the people of God, does not necessarily suggest that they have no further role.

Likewise, it is not helpful to list all of the places where the church or the Gentiles become heirs to promises made to Israel. There is no question that there are examples of this. These examples, however, do not prove that all of the promises to Israel will find fulfillment in the church, nor that the promises find their complete, or final, fulfillment in the church.[22]

Lacking clear statements in the New Testament, it is incumbent on us to go back to the Old Testament to discover what light may be shed on the issue. What did the eschatology of Israel look like? The principal source for Israel's eschatology is in the so-called aftermath oracles of the prophets. An aftermath oracle is defined as an oracle that is intended to convey to the people of Israel what plans God has for them in the aftermath of the coming or present covenant crisis. It is construed in response to the opinion, either real or hypothetical, that God has forgotten, abandoned, or rejected them. Typically it addresses what God will do to, or for, the nation Israel with regard to the future of their covenant relationship in the aftermath of their being exiled from the land.

In my study of the aftermath oracles of the Old Testament I have identified 122 distinct oracles. These are distributed fairly evenly through the period of classical prophecy.[23] The content of these oracles may be divided into four major categories and nearly forty subcategories. As might be expected there is some degree of overlapping. The breakdown is shown on the accompanying chart.

The category entitled "covenant" includes those elements that either refer to the covenant by definition, or are the direct promises of the covenant (land, people, king). The other three categories contain the elements that, for the most part, are implications or results of the covenant relationship. There are political, spiritual, and socioeconomic ramifications of the covenant that come in the form of benefits. What this indicates is that Israel's eschatology is entirely covenant oriented. Their expectations of the future are all premised on the covenant. By far the most frequently addressed subcategory is the land. Beyond that, of most interest for the question we are address-ing is the category containing the political aspects of the aftermath oracles.

The new covenant is an aftermath covenant. That is, it is proclaimed and described in aftermath oracles (Jer. 31–34; Isa. 61; Hos. 2; Ezek. 16; 34; 37) and is fully integrated with the content of the aftermath oracles. Hosea 2:18–23 is a good example:

> 18"In that day I will make a covenant for them
>   with the beasts of the field and the birds of the air
>   and the creatures that move along the ground.
> Bow and sword and battle
>   I will abolish from the land,
>   so that all may lie down in safety.
> 19I will betroth you to me forever;
>   I will betroth you in righteousness and justice,
>   in love and compassion.
> 20I will betroth you in faithfulness,
>   and you will acknowledge the LORD.
>
> 21"In that day I will respond,"
>   declares the LORD—
> "I will respond to the skies,
>   and they will respond to the earth;
> 22and the earth will respond to the grain,
>   the new wine and oil,
>   and they will respond to Jezreel.
> 23I will plant her for myself in the land;
>   I will show my love to the one I called
>   'Not my loved one.'
> I will say to those called 'Not my people,'
>   'You are my people';
>   and they will say, 'You are my God.' "

While some might be reluctant to identify this with the new covenant in Jeremiah, it is unarguably an aftermath covenant and contains most of the elements that are included in other

articulations of the aftermath covenant. Most significant here is
verse 23, which includes the replanting in the land and a
reelection of Israel. Also it should be noticed that these
exigencies are not conditioned on any particular response by
Israel. Additionally, some passages make it quite clear that this
will be an inviolable agreement.

> 4"Do not be afraid; you will not suffer shame.
>   Do not fear disgrace; you will not be humiliated.
> You will forget the shame of your youth
>   and remember no more the reproach of your
>   widowhood.
> 5For your Maker is your husband—
>   the LORD Almighty is his name—
>   the Holy One of Israel is your Redeemer;
> he is called the God of all the earth.
> 6The LORD will call you back
>   as if you were a wife deserted and distressed
>   in spirit—
> a wife who married young,
>   only to be rejected," says your God.
> 7"For a brief moment I abandoned you,
>   but with deep compassion I will bring you back.
>   8In a surge of anger
>   I hid my face from you for a moment,
> but with everlasting kindness
>   I will have compassion on you,"
>   says the LORD your Redeemer.
>
> 9"To me this is like the days of Noah,
>   when I swore that the waters of Noah
>   would never again cover the earth.
> So now I have sworn not to be angry with you,
>   never to rebuke you again.
> 10Though the mountains be shaken
>   and the hills be removed,
> yet my unfailing love for you will not be shaken
>   nor my covenant of peace be removed,"
>   says the LORD, who has compassion on you.
> (Isa. 54:4–10)

The overall thrust of the aftermath oracles clearly favors the restoration of a physical kingdom. John Sailhamer reaches the same conclusion as a result of his detailed study of Isaiah 2:

> Isaiah's visions of the future looked to a time when the Davidic kingship would be restored in Jerusalem and the Messiah would reign over that kingdom and rule all the nations of the world. In other words, they look to a time that fits remarkably well with John's vision of the earthly reign of Christ in Revelation 20. Taken at face value Isaiah's visions appear to speak of a literal fulfillment in Jerusalem itself and thus are not easily pressed into a reference to the establishment of the church.[24]

Some may contend that the opportunity for these oracles to be fulfilled in ethnic Israel occurred in the return from the Exile, and that those privileges have since been forfeited. This contention, however, would be much more difficult to defend concerning the oracles in Zechariah.

> [7]This is what the LORD Almighty says: "I will save my people from the countries of the east and the west. [8]I will bring them back to live in Jerusalem; they will be my people, and I will be faithful and righteous to them as their God." (Zech. 8:7–8)

A few chapters later:

:3350 [6]"I will strengthen the house of Judah
        and save the house of Joseph.
I will restore them
        because I have compassion on them.
They will be as though
        I had not rejected them,
for I am the LORD their God
        and I will answer them.
[7]The Ephraimites will become like mighty men,
        and their hearts will be glad as with wine.
Their children will see it and be joyful;
        their hearts will rejoice in the LORD.
[8]I will signal for them
        and gather them in.
Surely I will redeem them;

they will be as numerous as before.
9Though I scatter them among the peoples,
        yet in distant lands they will remember me.
They and their children will survive,
        and they will return.
10I will bring them back from Egypt
        and gather them from Assyria.
I will bring them to Gilead and Lebanon,
        and there will not be room enough for them.
11They will pass through the sea of trouble;
        the surging sea will be subdued
        and all the depths of the Nile will dry up.
Assyria's pride will be brought down
        and Egypt's scepter will pass away.
12I will strengthen them in the LORD
        and in his name they will walk,"
                declares the LORD. (Zech. 10:6–12)

The Old Testament speaks quite clearly on the issue when
it is talking about election being open at some future time to
those who were not elect along with Israel (e.g., Isa. 19:25).
How then can we conclude that other prophecies such as this,
which speak so specifically to Israel's situation are to find their
fulfillment in the Gentiles/church? The contrast is clear in
passages such as Isaiah 49:5–6 where the restoration of Israel is
pictured *alongside* the extension of salvation to the Gentiles, but
is *not equated to it.*[25]

5And now the LORD says—
        he who formed me in the womb to be his servant
to bring Jacob back to him
        and gather Israel to himself,
for I am honored in the eyes of the LORD
        and my God has been my strength—
6he says:
"It is too small a thing for you to be my servant
        to restore the tribes of Jacob
        and bring back those of Israel I have kept.
I will also make you a light for the Gentiles,
        that you may bring my salvation to the ends
        of the earth."

Some Reformed theologians have also recognized this distinct eschatological categorization in the Old Testament prophecies. Willem VanGemeren observes:

> Whenever they speak of the spiritual unity of Jews and Gentiles they reserve a prominent place for the Jews in the kingdom. Isaiah, for example, portrays the glory that will come to the Jews at the coming of the Redeemer, when the nations will come to their light (59:20; 60:1-3).[26]

This distinction is also maintained in the New Testament. In the famous grafting illustration in Romans 11, the tree represents ethnic Israel and the branches that have been pruned are the unfaithful (since the remnant have not been pruned). The Gentiles represent the grafted-in branches, but Paul speaks of the pruned-off branches as being yet able to be grafted in (vv. 23-24). Thus it is anticipated that unfaithful Israel still has a role in inheriting the promises, but can only do so in accepting the new situation. Though there are passages in which the New Testament authors apply some of the Israelite terminology to the church, and some in which promises made to Israel are shown to have spiritual analogs within the experience of the church, there are no clear examples of the New Testament's offering an interpretation by means of which the promises to Israel are spiritualized and realized completely by the church.[27]

One of the key passages used to defend a spiritualization of the promise of the land is Hebrews 11:13-16. Here the author of Hebrews contends that the faith of the ancient worthies stands as evidence to the fact that they sought a "heavenly country." While this statement might suggest a prioritization in the mind of Abraham and his spiritual "seed," it does not insist on an exclusively spiritual view. Certainly Abraham also expected a physical country and was told by God that such a land would belong to him (Gen. 15:13-21). Consequently passages such as Hebrews 11 must not be used to dismiss the expectation of a physical land in so cavalier a manner.

Some have understood Paul's silence with regard to the land as a clear indication that his eschatology and ecclesiology are "a-territorial." So W. D. Davies, in his classic investigation of the concept of "land," feels justified in concluding: "In the Christological logic of Paul, the land, like the Law, particular and provisional, had become irrelevant."[28] His position is clarified a few pages further on demonstrating that this irrelevance concerns the new people of God.

> The logic of Paul's Christology and missionary practice, then, seems to demand that the people of Israel living in the land had been replaced as the people of God by a universal community which had no special territorial attachment.[29]

Certainly I agree that the land is not an expected inheritance, nor a delineating factor for the redefined people of God. Nonetheless, this does not rule out a continued significance to the land for faithful, national Israel. All that it does is remove it as a significant feature for the soteric people of God.

The destiny of the believing remnant of Israel has not been totally subsumed by the destiny of the people of God. Though they share the destiny of the universal soteric people of God, the believing remnant of Israel also continue to have a destiny of their own that is linked to their previous role. This does not make them a separate people of God, but it distinguishes them within the people of God—a distinction that does not make them better and does not affect their standing in Christ (for good or ill), because in Christ there is neither Jew nor Gentile. This latter statement refers to their standing in Christ, not to the elimination of any distinction whatsoever. This point is pursued by Robert Saucy.

> Thus the unification of Gentile and Jew in the church does not rule out the possibility of *functional* distinctions between Israel and the other nations in the future, even as there are functional distinctions among believers in the church today without impairing spiritual equality.[30]

Male and female are still different, slaves are still differentiated from free in very important ways, but in Christ they are one. Therefore, Galatians 3:28 does not rule out a continuing destiny for Israel as a distinguishable subset within the newly constituted people of God, the spiritual seed of Abraham. That Paul should be silent on the matter of Israel's continuing destiny is not unusual given the focus of his ministry on the redefined people of God.

> The real centre of his interest has moved from "the land," concentrated in Jerusalem, to the communities "in Christ." This is what the Pauline epistles as a whole attest. Passages that deal directly with eschatology in its apocalyptic form are few. Paul's epistles are mostly peppered, not with apocalyptic imagery, but with terms such as "in Christ," "dying and rising with Christ," "in the Spirit." The life "in Christ" is the life of the eschatological Israel, an Israel, which, through Christ, transcends the connection with the land and with the Law attached to that land.[31]

Even Davies recognizes, however, that this shift does not negate any significance of the land, but merely subordinates it.

> It is arguable that [Paul] never completely and consciously and emotionally abandoned the geography of eschatology: it may have continued alongside his new awareness of the "ecclesiological" eschatology inaugurated by Christ. For a long time Paul apparently felt no incongruity between retaining his apocalyptic geography, centred in Jerusalem, even though, since he was "in Christ," it had become otiose. Theologically he had no longer any need of it: his geographical identity was subordinated to that of being "in Christ," in whom was neither Jew nor Greek.[32]

The astute reader will notice that this discussion has been conducted without discussion of whose hermeneutics are more biblical. I have neither glibly associated the Old Testament promises of land and kingdom with the millennium, nor have I advocated that millennial theology in the New Testament supersedes fulfillment of promises to ethnic Israel. These are emotionally charged issues that unfortunately often represent entrenchments. Certainly where New Testament teaching offers revision of Old Testament proclamations, we must yield to the New Testament. Nevertheless, we cannot summarily dismiss the Old Testament as virtually irrelevant. I am convinced that the model here proposed offers an opportunity to take the Old Testament seriously while at the same time adopting wholeheartedly the spiritual revisions and unanticipated fulfillments articulated by the New Testament.

SUMMARY

Walter Kaiser has identified three major types of theology that describe the relationship between Israel and the church. His convenient summary is worth quoting in full.

> 1. The *new Israel* view holds that geopolitical, national Israel was replaced by the church, which is now the new, spiritual Israel. There is no need to wait for any material or physical aspects to the fulfillment of God's promises to the patriarchs and David, or to expect a physical and real presence of Christ as he reigns from Jerusalem over all nations, for there will be no millennium.
>
> 2. The *covenant* view maintains that Israel and the church are one and the same throughout all of history: namely, they are the faithful from all of humanity. This one body is embraced in a covenant, not precisely referred to in Scripture, but surely one that embodies the essence of salvation described in the Bible: namely, the "covenant of grace" or the "covenant of redemption." All the promises, covenants, and prophecies are fulfilled in the gospel, which gospel is climaxed in the church, as God's covenant people. Thus individual believing Jews are grafted into the church.
>
> 3. The traditional *dispensational* view holds that Israel and the church have separate and distinct identities, destinies, and promises. During the so-called church age, Israel as a nation has been set aside, and the program of God has gone into a parenthesis or an intercalation. After this church age parenthesis comes to an end, God will resume relations with the nation Israel once again and restore the Davidic kingdom to its greatest height ever.[33]

Kaiser does not agree with any of these traditional views, which he elsewhere labels Replacement Covenant, Super Covenant, and Separate Covenant respectively.[34] He prefers the model of the Renewed Covenant.

In the main, this view agrees with the distinction between Israel and the church. But instead of continuing to say, as classical dispensationalism did, that there are two separate peoples (Israel and the church) with two separate programs (the earthly kingdom and the heavenly kingdom of our Lord), this view stresses that there is one people ("the people of God") with a number of discernable aspects within that one people (such as Israel and the church), and there is only one program of God (the "kingdom of God") with numerous aspects under that single program.[35]

The model that I am proposing finds little in this statement by Kaiser to disagree with. Although the view of Israel is therefore very similar, the primary difference remains on the essence of the covenant. Kaiser's position is that the promise is central to the essence and purpose of the covenant, while my model places more emphasis on revelation.

As is eminently clear in the new dispensationalism presented in Blaising and Bock (*Dispensationalism, Israel and the Church* (Grand Rapids: Zondervan, 1992), an inaugurated eschatology of some sort is now accepted by all the major systems, and the present model is no exception. I include in the "not yet" portions the physical promises that have yet to be claimed by a believing Israel.

Given the proposed model of the revelatory purpose of the covenant, I have suggested that the issue of conditionality is a moot point because it deals with what is over and done. There is no need to view Israel as having been rejected as the people of God once we accept the view that the concept of the people of God has undergone a radical transformation by being redefined under the terms of the new covenant. Though this redefinition has occurred, there is still continuity on a number of levels with the previous phases, leading to the conclusion that ethnic Israel will yet respond with belief and inherit the land promised to Abraham and play an important role in the kingdom of God.

NOTES

[1]N. T. Wright, *The Climax of the Covenant* (Minneapolis: Fortress, 1991), 14.
[2]Ibid., 148–49.
[3]Ibid., 36. Although Wright makes many statements such as these that offer support for the case that I am making, it will be obvious to those familiar with Wright's work that we are not in total agreement in a number of related areas.
[4]R. L. Saucy, *The Case for Progressive Dispensationalism* (Grand Rapids: Zondervan, 1993), 189.
[5]N. T. Wright, *The Climax of the Covenant*, 47. The case for the church as the people of God is argued very ably in Hans LaRondelle, *The Israel of God in Prophecy* (Berrien Springs: Andrews University Press, 1983), 104-21. Many of the points made by LaRondelle criticizing traditional dispensationalism have been recognized by the new dispensationalism and revised. I find myself in agreement with many of the positions he argues for, though he is not reluctant to maintain that the church has replaced Israel, terminology that I find unwarranted.
[6]Ibid., 245–46. My difference here with Wright is that I see the intended goal as being somewhat broader, though he speaks of the goal that Paul is developing in Romans, with which I have no disagreement.
[7]Robert Saucy, "Israel and the Church: A Case for Discontinuity" in *Continuity and Discontinuity*, ed. John S. Fienberg (Wheaton: Crossway, 1988), 258.
[8]N. T. Wright, *The Climax of the Covenant*, 246.
[9]Ibid., 249–50.
[10]Hans LaRondelle, *The Israel of God in Prophecy*, 127.
[11]S. Lewis Johnson, "Evidence From Romans 9–11," in *A Case For Premillennialism*, ed. D. K. Campbell and J. L. Townsend (Chicago: Moody Press, 1992), 199–223; R. L. Saucy, *The Case for Progressive Dispensationalism*, 250–63.
[12]Bruce Waltke, "Kingdom Promises as Spiritual," in *Continuity and Discontinuity*, 273.
[13]Ibid., 274–75.
[14]A convenient and fairly comprehensive defense of the biblical support for the position that anticipates a physical kingdom on earth can be found in D. K. Campbell and J. L. Townsend, *A Case for Premillennialism: A New Consensus*.
[15]D. A. Carson, "Matthew" in *The Expositor's Bible Commentary*, vol. 8., ed. F. Gaebelein (Grand Rapids: Zondervan, 1984), 203.
[16]Ibid., 454.
[17]For some recent discussions see James Barr, *Biblical Words For Time* (London: SCM, 1969), 73–74, 93, 123–24; D. Howard "The Case for Kingship in the Old Testament Narrative Books and the Psalms" *TJ* 9 (1988): 29n.38; Allan MacRae, "'olam" in *Theological Wordbook of the Old Testament*, vol. II, eds. R. L. Harris, Gleason Archer, Bruce Waltke (Chicago: Moody Press, 1980), 672 (#1631). Commenting specifically on the use of this term with regard to the

continuing validity of the law see D. Moo in *The Law, the Gospel and the Modern Christian: Five Views,* ed. W. Strickland (Grand Rapids: Zondervan, 1993), 348.

[18]A. Jepsen, cited by E. W. Nicholson, *God and His People* (Oxford: Clarendon Press, 1986), 89.

[19]N. T. Wright, *The Climax of the Covenant,* 181.

[20]L. S. Chafer, *Systematic Theology,* vol. IV (Dallas: Dallas Theological Seminary, 1947), 47–48.

[21]Bruce A. Ware, "The New Covenant and the People(s) of God" in *Dispensationalism, Israel and the Church,* ed. C. A. Blaising and D. L. Bock (Grand Rapids: Zondervan, 1992), 96–97.

[22]G. E. Ladd, "Historic Premillennialism" in *The Meaning of the Millennium,* ed. R. G. Clouse (Downers Grove: InterVarsity Press, 1977), 28.

[23]Assyrian period: 40; Babylonian period: 47; Postexilic period: 35. See the chart on page 135.

[24]John Sailhamer, "Evidence From Isaiah 2" in *A Case For Premillennialism,* 101.

[25]See Saucy, *The Case for Progressive Dispensationalism,* 125.

[26]W. VanGemeren, "Israel as the Hermeneutical Crux in the Interpretation of Prophecy" *WTJ* 46 (1984): 285. VanGemeren spends ten pages of this article (284–94) defending a future expectation (in a material sense) for the Jews who believe. Much of his support is drawn from traditional Reformed writers. It is interesting to see how much nearer Reformed and dispensational thinking are drawing to one another on this issue. Likewise see the mediating position of D. Fuller who reflects this view in *Gospel and Law: Contrast or Continuum?* (Grand Rapids: Eerdmans, 1980), 133–34.

[27]A thorough analysis of the pertinent passages was done by R. C. Walton, "The Relationship Between Israel and the Church in Scripture" (Th.M. thesis, Westminster Theological Seminary, 1975).

[28]W. D. Davies, *The Gospel and the Land* (Berkeley: University of California Press, 1974), 179.

[29]Ibid., 182.

[30]Robert L. Saucy, "The Church as the Mystery of God" in *Dispensationalism, Israel and the Church,* 155.

[31]W. D. Davies, *The Gospel and the Land,* 217.

[32]Ibid., 220.

[33]Walter C. Kaiser, "An Epangelical Response" in *Dispensationalism, Israel and the Church,* 360.

[34]Ibid., 364–66.

[35]Ibid., 367.

9

COVENANT IN THE TESTAMENTS

COVENANT AND CANON

In the model proposed in this book the covenant has been viewed as the primary mechanism in God's program of revelation. This approach to the covenant has been identified as a biblical-theology approach because it has attempted to understand the diachronic development of the covenant concept and the revelatory program. One of the perpetual questions resounding throughout the discipline of biblical theology and, specifically Old Testament theology, is whether or not there is a center—a unifying concept. The problem and its ramifications have been well-articulated by Walter Kaiser.

> Simply stated, the real problem is this: Does a key exist for an orderly and progressive arrangement of the subjects, themes, and teachings of the OT? And here is the most crucial and sensitive question of all: Were the writers of the OT consciously aware of such a key as they continued to add to the historical stream of revelation?
>
> The answer to these questions will literally determine the destiny and direction of OT theology. If no such key can be demonstrated inductively from the text, and if the writers were not deliberately writing out of such an awareness, then we shall have to be content with talking about the different theologies of the OT. Consequently, the idea of an OT theology as such must be permanently abandoned. Not only

would it be necessary to acknowledge that there was no
unity to be found in the OT, but the search for the legitimate
and authoritative lines of continuity with the NT would need
to be abandoned as well.[1]

Perhaps, however, this is too facile a proposition. Is it
really true that the unity of the Old Testament or the unity of
the Bible depends on the identification of a central key? Is it not
possible that the Old Testament is unified by a common
purpose rather than by a central theme?

Revelation as the Purpose of the OT

By definition and by creedal assertion, the common
unifying purpose of the Bible is to reveal God. It is to be
expected that our infinitely sophisticated and multifaceted God
would require every literary genre available and would need to
delve into a wide range of topics in order to provide a
sufficiently adequate data base for us to enter into a relationship
with him. It is this purpose that served as the canonical engine
for the authors, editors, and canonizers of the Old Testament.
A key theme would arguably be too restrictive. A center is not
necessary in order for the unity of the Old Testament or the
Bible as a whole to be maintained. Unity of purpose is more
essential than unity of theme.

Covenant: The Canonical Center of the OT?

We have already mentioned in chapter 1 the proposal by
Walther Eichrodt that covenant should be viewed as the center
of Old Testament theology. Like most theories concerning the
center of OT theology, Eichrodt's theory founders in the shoals
of the wisdom literature where the covenant is rarely mentioned, and is certainly not central.[2] It is important to understand that there is a necessary distinction that must be
maintained between revelation and covenant. While the covenant is the primary mechanism of God's revelatory program,
and all special revelation comes through Israel by virtue of her
covenant agreement with God, not all special revelation is
related to the covenant. This distinction is central to an

understanding of the respective roles of historical literature, which is thoroughly covenant-oriented, and wisdom literature, which makes very sparse reference to the covenant.

No one in the ancient world doubted that deity directed the events of history. But it is much more difficult to deduce confidently just what any particular god was doing and what his purposes were (if, indeed, his actions were purposeful). Consequently, the events of history could be identified as general revelation. The historical literature of the Old Testament is special revelation that clarifies what is properly extracted from the otherwise general revelation of divine involvement in human events. It explains what God is doing and why he is doing it. This literature is closely related to the covenant because the special revelation focuses on events pertaining to Israel.

Another area of divine activity accepted by consensus in the ancient world was the ordering of the cosmos and society. Like historical events, aspects of the order in the cosmos and in society could be subject to misinterpretation. It was assumed that deity was involved, but what was actually being communicated? Wisdom literature is special revelation that clarifies what is properly extracted from the otherwise general revelation of the divine establishment of order in the cosmos and in society. This literature is less related to the covenant because human behavior and the operation of the cosmos are, by definition, broader in scope and, to a greater degree, common to all peoples. In this way revelation can be seen to be a unifying purpose, common to both historical and wisdom literature, while the covenant, though a mechanism of revelation, is not an essential ingredient of all revelation. I conclude that there is neither reason nor sufficient evidence for considering the covenant to be the canonical center for Old Testament theology.

The covenant is the central mechanism of revelation and, as such, is one of the most important themes of the Old Testament, arguably *the* most important. This does not make it the center, for as the canonical center it would need to be the intentional subject matter of each of the authors of Old Testament Scripture. The fact that it does not serve as the unifying feature of all of the Old Testament does not mitigate the unifying contribution that it does provide. The link between Torah, historical literature, and prophetic literature is supplied by the covenant.

THE COVENANT IN THE NEW TESTAMENT
Christ and the Covenant

The only specific reference to the covenant that Jesus makes in the Gospels is in the words at the Last Supper that the cup was the new covenant of his blood (Matt. 26:28; Mark 14:24; Luke 22:20). Nonetheless, the covenant is central to his teaching. Jesus preached the kingdom of God throughout his ministry, and the kingdom cannot be understood apart from the covenant. Likewise he makes frequent reference to the law—viewing himself as the focal point of both the kingdom and the law.

Granting then that Jesus understood his own role as being intimately connected to the covenant phases, can anything be said about his view of the purpose or function of the covenant?

A number of Jesus' parables and illustrations address the old *versus* the new (Matt. 13:52; Luke 5:36–39). In each the indication is that both be retained but that they should not be confused or mixed together. This accords with our hypothesis concerning the covenant, but it is not altogether clear that Jesus is specifically addressing the covenant in these passages.[3]

Paul's View of the Covenant—2 Corinthians 3:4–18

Certainly Paul's most explicit treatment of the covenant is found in 2 Corinthians 3:4–18.

> [4]Such confidence as this is ours through Christ before God. [5]Not that we are competent in ourselves to claim anything for ourselves, but our competence comes from God. [6]He has made us competent as ministers of a new covenant—not of the letter but of the Spirit; for the letter kills, but the Spirit gives life.
>
> [7]Now if the ministry that brought death, which was engraved in letters on stone, came with glory, so that the

Israelites could not look steadily at the face of Moses because of its glory, fading though it was, 8will not the ministry of the Spirit be even more glorious? 9If the ministry that condemns men is glorious, how much more glorious is the ministry that brings righteousness! 10For what was glorious has no glory now in comparison with the surpassing glory. 11And if what was fading away came with glory, how much greater is the glory of that which lasts!

12Therefore, since we have such a hope, we are very bold. 13We are not like Moses, who would put a veil over his face to keep the Israelites from gazing at it while the radiance was fading away. 14But their minds were made dull, for to this day the same veil remains when the old covenant is read. It has not been removed, because only in Christ is it taken away. 15Even to this day when Moses is read, a veil covers their hearts. 16But whenever anyone turns to the Lord, the veil is taken away. 17Now the Lord is the Spirit, and where the Spirit of the Lord is, there is freedom. 18And we, who with unveiled faces all reflect the Lord's glory, are being transformed into his likeness with ever-increasing glory, which comes from the Lord, who is the Spirit.

One of the significant issues concerning this passage is that it uses the terminology "old covenant" (v. 14) in contrast to the "new covenant" (v. 6). The distinctive feature of this new covenant is that it operates by means of the Spirit within, a concept that is related by Paul (v. 3) to Jeremiah 31. The reference to tablets of stone (v.3) shows that by the "old" covenant Paul is referring to the Law. How much discontinuity does such terminology demand? It is of interest here to note that the Old Covenant referred to is something that is read, most likely referring to the public reading of the Old Testament in the synagogue.[4] This is the only place in the New Testament where this terminology is used, and it has been speculated that Paul may have coined the expression "old covenant" as a counterpart to "new covenant."[5]

As Paul's "letters of recommendation" (2 Cor. 3:2) the Corinthian believers are bearing witness to the glory of the new covenant. So also verse eighteen speaks of the believer as "reflecting the Lord's glory" by being transformed by the Spirit.

How is this "revelatory" function different from that which is found in the previous phases? In the Old Testament the extent to which any Israelite achieved holiness was not in itself the special revelation. The law was the special revelation and it allowed, indeed urged, the Israelites to reflect God's holiness. Their revelatory function was served in that the law came to (through) them. The anticipated result was obedience, godliness (godlikeness), and relationship. Although they could testify to the character of God through their lives, their lives did not constitute special revelation. This is no less true for New Testament believers. By being Christlike we reflect our Lord's glory and we bring honor to him. But Christ is the special revelation, not our lives. There is a revelatory aspect to this godlikeness, but it cannot be identified as special revelation.

When Israel is identified as a light to the nations, both of the above aspects of revelation could be included. They are an instrument of God's special revelation and thereby serve as a beacon for God. Additionally, their conduct is to be a testimony to the character of God. The New Testament carries over the same metaphor for believers (Matt. 5:14) and also includes both aspects.

The Remainder of the NT—Hebrews 8-10

Hebrews 8 discusses the superiority of the high priesthood of Christ. As a superior high priest, the author also presents Christ as the mediator of a "better covenant" (v. 6). His evidence for such a statement comes through the citation of several Old Testament texts that highlight some of the better promises. It is not that the "first" covenant was defective. The new covenant is a better covenant because it has better promises, as identified in Jeremiah 31. Specifically, then, the law in the heart and the forgiveness of sins distinguish the new covenant as being better. The new covenant offers advantages not previously available. The author does not address the purpose or function of the covenant in the Old Testament. The soteriological shortcomings of the sacrificial system noted by the author of Hebrews (ch. 10) do not reflect any belief that the old covenant intrinsically had a soteric purpose. It was only

because Jewish interpretation had attributed a soteric function
to the law that its soteric faults needed to be demonstrated.
Before this discussion can be completed, closer attention
must be given to 8:13. "By calling this covenant 'new,' he has
made the first one obsolete; and what is obsolete and aging will
soon disappear." The interpretations of the terms here translated "obsolete" and "disappear" are significant to our subject.
It becomes clear in Hebrews 9–10 that the author is considering
the covenant in terms of its providing a means of relationship to
God. He insists that with the availability of the new covenant,
there is no longer the option of relating to God on the old
terms. Christ is the new Torah, and therefore the Torah only
functions by means of the law of Christ that is understood to be
superimposed on it. This does not mean that the purpose of the
old covenant (in this model, revelation) is obsolete. None of the
New Testament authors would deny the ongoing validity of
Old Testament revelation (e.g., Rom. 15:4; 2 Tim. 3:16–17). But
relationship to God by means of an Old Testament understanding alone will not suffice. That is what is obsolete and soon to
disappear all together.

In conclusion it must be admitted that the majority of
discussion on the covenant in the New Testament focuses on
the issue of salvation. This is not surprising since this was the
essence of the revelation and election in the new covenant
phase. The revelatory program had eventuated in a program of
salvation. But while the New Testament authors are willing to
discuss salvation as it had recently become available in contrast
to what was provided or understood in the Old Testament,
they do not impose a soteric purpose on the covenant in the
Old Testament. If anything, they argue that it was never
constructed in such a way to deal with salvation in any long-
range or permanent sense.

New Covenant and New Testament

The terminology *Old Testament* and *New Testament* comes
over from the Latin designations where *testamentum* is a more
accurate rendering of the Greek *diatheke* than is our English
word *testament*. Thus our English terminology actually reflects a

tradition of dividing the canon between the "old covenant" and the "new covenant."[6] These designations portray the same concept as is being espoused in this book. The revelation of God by means of the old covenant is comprised of all the covenant phases prior to Christ, while the revelation of God by means of the new covenant focuses on the provision of salvation and all that is made available through Christ. There are two canonical divisions and there are two covenants, separate yet organically related as are the two divisions of Scripture. There is not a new covenant because the old one failed or was broken. The new covenant phase was part of the plan from the beginning. It does not replace the old, it completes it.

> Apart from the organic unity of the Old Testament with the New, which makes it an indispensable part of the Christian canon, the Old Testament makes in various ways its own distinctive contribution to the volume of revelation. The supreme *religious* value of the Old Testament is the way in which it presents God as the Living God, One who is dynamically alive and active in self-revelation, not simply the Prime Mover or Pure Actuality of certain schools of philosophy, nor yet merely the Self-Existent Being. He is that, of course, but He is much more. He is the God of creation, providence and redemption; He is the God who makes Himself known in the mighty acts with which He breaks into the course of history. And this picture of God in the Old Testament prepares us for the supremely redemptive mighty act which He wrought in sending His Son into the world for our deliverance and in raising Him from the dead.[7]

NOTES

[1]Walter C. Kaiser, *Toward an Old Testament Theology* (Grand Rapids: Zondervan, 1978), 20–21.

[2]In Kenneth Barker's helpful summary he rightly observes that "most statements of a theological center are too limited (e.g., promise or covenant), too broad (e.g., God), or too anthropocentric (e.g., redemption or salvation history)" ("The Scope and Center of Old and New Testament Theology and Hope" in *Dispensationalism, Israel and the Church*, ed. C. A. Blaising and D. L. Bock [Grand Rapids: Zondervan, 1992], 305–6; pp. 305–18 for the complete discussion).

[3]*TDNT* 5: 718.
[4]*TDNT* 5: 719.
[5]*TDNT* 5: 720n.13.
[6]F. F. Bruce, *The Books and the Parchments*, 5th ed. (Westwood, N.J.: Revell, 1963), 76.
[7]Ibid., 85–86.

10

THE LAW AND THE COVENANT

Having discussed the nature and purpose of the covenant, we are now in a position to assess the role that the law plays within that covenant framework. Questions concerning the continuing relevance of the law were at the forefront of discussions between Christ and the Pharisees and were among the largest issues to be resolved by the early church. Such questions also arise from among the most problematic of the exegetical controversies of New Testament studies. Theological camps are defined by this issue both in terms of theory and in practical issues of lifestyle. Is the law relevant today? If it is part of God's revelation, how can it be set aside? How could something have been right then and not now, if God does not change? To answer these questions we shall have to go the long way around and start with the basic foundational understanding of what the law is and, most importantly, how it relates to the covenant.

THE ORIGINS OF LAW IN ISRAEL

When God said to the Israelites at Mt. Sinai, "Thou shalt not kill (murder)," were they startled at the innovation and stunned by how that would change their way of life? When God gave them regulations for sacrifice, was he initiating a whole new institution? No. Murder was prohibited in all societies and would have been contrary to law among the

Israelite tribes during their centuries of life in Egypt. Sacrifice was regularly practiced both throughout the ancient world and by Israel itself long before the Exodus. Israel had legislation by which their society was governed and guidelines that regulated their worship from the very beginning. We would assume that such legislation would have looked very much like the legislation that has survived from the ancient world, preserved in the laws of Hammurabi, Eshnunna, and the like. Furthermore, many of the laws preserved in the Pentateuch show a striking resemblance to laws that are preserved in other ancient Near Eastern sources.[1]

What, then, is God doing at Sinai? Is he giving Israel legislation? If it is very similar to the legislation that they were already operating under as well as common to legislation of other contemporary societies, what is the point? To answer we must ask about the function of the legal sections of the Pentateuch. This is best approached by starting with the function of the legal collections of the ancient Near East.

THE FUNCTION OF LEGAL COLLECTIONS

A consensus has been developing for the last several decades, and is now firmly in place, that the extant legal collections from the ancient Near East are academic and literary in nature, rather than juridical or legislative.[2] That is to say, they describe parts of the law (within a literary framework) rather than prescribe what the law should be.[3] It is from the literary framework that a determination must be made concerning the purpose for which the legal material has been gathered together.

The prologues and epilogues of the ancient collections show them to be attempts to demonstrate that the administration in power was properly discharging its responsibility to provide and maintain justice in society.[4] The basis of the relationship between the king and the gods was that the king would be granted the authority to rule and that he, in return, would rule justly. The gods were the guardians of the cosmic law that was built into the fabric of the natural world. As guardians they granted authority to human kings to make laws that would reflect the cosmic order of things.[5] The law collections served as the king's defense that he was doing just that. They were comprised of *illustrations* of the kind of laws that were enacted and/or enforced under the king's administration. By collecting such exemplary laws the king intended to reveal something about himself as the promulgator of those laws. He was under obligation to promulgate and enforce such laws so as to retain his official relationship with the gods under whose auspices he ruled.

In a very similar manner, the biblical law collections are comprised of illustrations of legislation paradigms that are intended to reveal something about the promulgator of the laws.[6] A key difference here, however, is that God is the promulgator of law in Israel.[7] Therefore, rather than revealing the justice of the king, the law in Israel reveals the holiness of God. The law is a revelation of God's ways (Ps. 103:7). Beyond mandating justice for society, Yahweh mandates holiness for his people. Just as the king's enforcing that type of legislation maintained his elect relationship with the gods, so Israel's enforcing legislation would maintain their elect relationship with God.

The law reveals what God is like and circumscribes a covenant relationship that asks the people to imitate and reflect God's holiness.[8] The collections of laws are not intended to prescribe a comprehensive legislation, but represent the foundation for the ever-changing legislation required in order for a society to operate.[9] In that sense, it functioned more like our constitution, which is not legislation but the foundation for legislation. The obligatory force carried by the law in the Bible is not the obligatory force of enforceable legislation, but that of a binding agreement; the obligatory force is thus connected more to covenant than to law.[10] Shalom Paul captures this in his contrast between casuistic and apodictic law.

> Whereas casuistic law deals with precedent and what is, apodictic commandments express what must and ought to be. It addresses man a priori as to what is right or wrong. It is prescriptive not descriptive, prospective not retrospective,

absolute not relative, categorically imperative and obligatory
not conditional, subjective and personal not objective and
impersonal—God's will not man's. Its purpose is to shape
and form a society, not to state cases and provide remedies.
No time limit is placed on its demands. Sanctions are absent;
yet it appeals to the conscience of the individual for constant
obedience and fidelity. It is preventive and precautionary,
obliging the responsibility of every member of the community. Hence, to impersonal legislation is added personal
obligation and commandment; to the formula is added
feeling; to the intellect, the heart; and to the letter of the law
is added the spirit and values of metajuristic principles—
together they constitute the charter of the people of Israel.[11]

Israel, as the covenant people, is obliged to observe the law
in order to maintain its elect status before God. That does not
mean that its legislation will always and only look exactly like
the law of the Pentateuch, for that law is illustrative. Its actual
legislation must reflect interpretation of the covenantal law.[12] So
Jacob Weingreen observes

> In ancient Israel, when it was found necessary to achieve
> some change in a biblical law, the jurists could not erase or
> ignore the original law in the inspired law code. They could
> attain their ends only by the application of established rules
> of exposition which, on the one hand, produced the
> modifications needed, while, on the other hand, the text of
> the original law remained unaltered.[13]

Indeed the ability of the new interpretive legislation (the
traditio) to have any claim of authority was based on its
connection to the authoritative covenantal text (the *traditum*).

> The authority of the legal exegesis propounded lies in its
> relationship to the *traditum*. The *mischgattung* [mixed genre]
> requires one to recognize that the human exegetical voice,
> the voice of *traditio*, is a subordinate voice. The divine
> *traditum* precedes each *traditio*, sets its course, and guaran-
> tees it religious-social authority. Thus, just as the legal
> exegeses in the Hebrew Bible are dominated by the genres in
> which they are found, the *traditum* has a hierarchical pre-
> eminence over each and every *traditio*. Indeed, the *traditio*

does not exist for its own sake, but solely for the sake of the *traditum* to which it is attached.[14]

So throughout the Old Testament, rulings and legislation are enacted through an attempt to apply covenantal law to contemporary situations.[15] From Jehoshaphat to Hezekiah, from Josiah to Ezra, it is evident that covenantal law is the foundation of, but not the sole normative expression of actual legislation.[16] This does not reduce its obligatory force, but rechannels it and restricts it to a sphere of operation within the covenant relationship.

THE LAW BEYOND THE OLD TESTAMENT

Just as had been done by many before them, the Pharisees had interpreted the covenantal law for their own society in light of their own understanding.

> When Israel adopted an understanding of God's law as a set
> of rules preserved in written texts, they were forced to
> develop an oral tradition to interpret legal texts according to
> the principles just outlined. The eternal laws of God,
> delivered to Moses once for all, had to be adapted, augment-
> ed, and rationalized in order to be used in meditation, piety,
> and jurisprudence. The emergence of this interpretive tradi-
> tion in post-exilic Judaism charted the course for Judaism and
> set the stage for the birth of Christianity.[17]

As undoubtedly had happened before, the contemporary interpretation of the law had come to be identified with the law, so that it was difficult to see the law except through the lens of its contemporary interpretation.[18] In this way the contemporary interpretation was not seen to supersede the law, but was rather superimposed on it and equated with it.

> The legal *traditio* would appear as that which explores and
> even reveals the full potential of the legal *traditum* to deal
> with new historical circumstances. In a word, an exegetical
> *traditio* faithful to the determinants of the *traditum* would be
> preserved and acknowledged as its true historical ally—not
> as an alien factor. Indeed, one may suspect that the tradents
> and draftsmen of ancient Israel, who preserved the *traditio* as

part of the *traditum*, may even have perceived the *traditio* as having some divine status from its very onset—if only in the sense that the *traditio* was understood as part of the full potential of the original legal revelation. For to the extent that the *traditum* was believed to make sense, and its formulations were considered valid, these had to make sense and be valid in all ways. Hence, obscurities in the *traditum* had to be clarified; its (real or apparent) implications drawn out; its incomprehensiveness supplemented; and its contradictions shown to be more apparent than real. From this perspective, the exegetical *traditio* is a task with sacred responsibilities, since it partakes of the power and authority of the divine *traditum* itself. There would thus develop, over many generations and with different rationales, the notion that the original written legal *traditum* may be—and often must be—supplemented by a legal exegetical *traditio* which is inspired by it, and that the continuous inspiration of the *traditum* upon its faithful exegetes is nothing other than the continuous revelation of God through that *traditum*.[19]

Examining first-century Judaism it becomes clear that in many ways the covenantal law had ceased to be an object of study in favor of the interpretation of the law that had been superimposed on it. Thus the rabbis studied and interpreted the rabbis rather than going all the way back to the covenantal law itself. This is demonstrated in the Mishnah (not compiled in writing until after Christ), which to a large extent represents contemporary Judaism.

> The Mishna . . . was endowed with undisputed authority. Since the Mishna was the only recognized authoritative exposition of the Torah, its influence was overriding, so much that it was given priority over the Bible it expounded.[20]

Such had become the power of the traditional interpretation.

When Jesus began interacting with the Jewish leaders, they were shocked at his neglect of their traditional interpretations. It was an act of audacity, in their view, for Jesus to bypass all of that time-honored tradition and offer his own interpretation of covenantal law. But what Jesus was doing, in effect, was replacing the superimposed rabbinic law with his own superim-

posed interpretation of covenantal law.[21] We see Jesus presenting himself as a new Torah that perfectly fulfills the covenantal
Torah.

> The inwardness of the New Covenant of Jeremiah's hope is
> achieved for Paul through the indwelling Christ, the New
> Torah "written in the heart." The Law within him is Christ in
> him; the indwelling Christ has replaced the old Torah written
> on tablets of stone and has become a Torah written within.[22]

Christ as the new Torah fulfills the covenantal Torah in the
sense that he carries out all that the former was ever meant to
be. The superimposed interpretations of the law were understood to carry authority insofar as they were understood as
accurate reflections of what the law was all about: i.e., offering
revelation of the character of God and maintaining a proper
relationship to God.

Christ is the new Torah within the new covenant. When an
ancient king had a vassal treaty with a neighboring king, and
that neighboring king died and was succeeded by his son, the
treaty would be renewed and redrawn. The basis of the treaty
may not have been radically changed, but there may have been
variations in the stipulations. In Christ, the covenant relationship is redefined, but the basic thrust of the covenant has not
changed. Now the character of God is revealed not through
legislative examples of how a godly person will act, but by
God's Son who came and lived among us. The map has been
replaced by a guide. That does not make the map wrong, but a
guide makes a map unnecessary.[23] The Sinai Torah covenant
had not been distinctly new in providing new laws, but
adopted much of the common law into a new framework—the
foundation being the revelation of God's character in the
relationship of the covenant. In the same way Christ's coming
and teaching were not distinctly new in providing different
law, but again adopted a new framework—the foundation
being the revelation of God in Christ in the relationship with
God available through the new covenant. The Spirit of Christ
indwelling us is the law in our hearts that was promised in the
new covenant (2 Cor. 3:3). Obedience to Christ is the new set

of stipulations in the renewed covenant. Obedience to the law of Christ satisfies the requirements of the law. This has been illustrated well by Stephen Westerholm.

> The instructor of an undergraduate music course in which a concert pianist enrolls may quickly—perhaps with some embarrassment—grant that the "student" has more than adequately "fulfilled" a number of requirements for the course even though the specific work normally demanded has not been done. Indeed, the accomplished musician views the exercises and norms imposed on beginners with a knowing detachment, recognizing their limitations as well as their pedagogic importance and feeling free to ignore what now hinders rather than promotes the making of music. Such a failure to follow the norms while nonetheless achieving their intended purpose should be distinguished from the stubborn refusal of a novice to be subject to a necessary discipline. The consummate musician "fulfills" the intention of the rules without always observing them; but the recalcitrant novice neither "does" nor "fulfills" the "law" of the musical trade.[24]

The Mosaic law has not been superseded, but the law of Christ has been superimposed on it. Just as Israel entered into a covenant relationship that was governed by law, so the Gentiles would enter into a covenant relationship governed by law—but the law in this new covenant is the law of Christ.

This understanding makes Christ's comments in Matthew 5:17–19 quite clear. The law is fulfilled in Christ. The law's purpose and function are carried out perfectly through the teachings and ministry of Jesus.

> Yet if the Torah was first and foremost the revelation of a personal God rather than a code of law, it is this new revelation of a personal God which alone can enable men to understand it truly and to obey it properly.[25]

Furthermore, in Christ's interpretation of the law, the law is seen in its best light and the spirit of the law is revealed. Yet, the statements that none of the law will pass away and that breaking of the law is a serious offense can now be appreciated as references to Christ's authoritative interpretation of the law.

> There is, therefore, no contradiction between a ruling of Jesus and the "letter of the Torah." There is no question of the authority of Jesus versus the authority of the Torah. There is only the question of true Torah (which in its "jot and tittle" can only agree with and testify to Wisdom) and false Torah (which for Matthew means the law falsely understood). Therefore, Jesus' teaching may on the one hand be proved from the law or on the other be asserted as sheer authoritative legal pronouncement. The Torah, when it is rightly understood, can only testify to itself. The "I say unto you" of Matthew 5 is not intended to abolish the law. It may, in a sense, extend and deepen the requirements of the law, but that is not its intent either. It is, instead, the authoritative declaration of what in fact the law is.[26]

His interpretation does not nullify or supersede, it is superimposed on and identified with the law of Moses.[27]

Once we proceed to Paul's use of the law we encounter the problem of potentially contradictory statements. Though many assume that these apparent differences can be reconciled, the logic to do so has often proved elusive.

> Scholars have so far been least successful in explaining this puzzling aspect of Paul's theology of the law—that is, how he can talk of Christians being removed from the sphere of the law while also sometimes quoting it with approval as the law they fulfill. It has at least become clear that many of the commonly accepted explanations do not hold up under close scrutiny. To say that Paul was working with an implicit distinction between ceremonial, civil and moral parts of the law is to impose an artificial distinction not only on the Old Testament law (is Sabbath law "ceremonial" or "moral"?) but also on Paul (in what category is food offered to idols?). To talk of a distinction between the law misused in legalism and the law rightly used as the will of God is, as Sanders has shown, wholly misleading. Both the Lutheran and Reformed approaches to this problem appear to reach a solution only by oversimplifying it and ignoring some of the awkward evidence: in Pauline ethics the law is not simply ignored and

abrogated (see 1 Cor. 9:8–10), but nor are all its dictates fully obeyed (see Rom. 14).[28]

Solutions explicating Paul's view of the law are many and the issue is complex.[29] Romans 10:4 is at the hub of this swirling controversy. N. Thomas Wright has offered this explanation with which I am inclined to agree:

> The notorious crux of 10:4 can, I think, be reduced to these terms: that the Torah is neither abolished as though it were bad or demonic, nor affirmed in the sense which the Jews took it. It was a good thing, given deliberately by God for a specific task and a particular period of time. When the task is done and the time is up, the Torah reaches its goal, which is also the conclusion of its intended reign, not because it was a bad thing to be abolished but because it was a good thing whose job is done. . . . The Messiah is the fulfillment of the long purposes of Israel's God. It was for this that Torah was given in the first place as a deliberately temporary mode of administration. In the Messiah are fulfilled the creator's paradoxical purposes for Israel and hence for the world. He is the climax of the covenant.[30]

Likewise the "condemning" aspect of the law may be understood in terms of the inability of fallen humankind to appropriate the law to the extent that it could effectuate salvation.[31]

> The Torah itself, it seems, is for Paul good, and even glorious, but in the event can only condemn its recipients, because of their state of heart. It is only, finally, when the work of Christ and the Spirit has been accomplished that the glory which shone in the Torah can shine once more, this time effectively.[32]

What did Paul refer to when he used the term *nomos* (law)? I agree with what appears to be the overall consensus, that he generally was speaking of the Mosaic law.[33] His criticism of the law was of the Pharisaic interpretation of the law (their *traditio*), which was purported to stand for the law itself (the *traditum*).[34] Additionally he objects to the soteric efficacy of conforming to the Pharisaic interpretation of the requirements of the law. This goes far beyond the external-internal dichotomy, which was too facile. Of the nine views of Paul and the law listed by Klyne Snodgrass this comes closest to number six, the view of Cranfield, though it is not necessary to refer to the Jewish view of the law as a misunderstanding.[35] The arguments of Dunn, Westerholm, Moo, and others who have all sufficiently demonstrated that one cannot assume that Paul is objecting to legalism only, are certainly valid.[36] Snodgrass has provided a very helpful list of affirmations that coincide with the view here espoused:

1. Paul never saw himself as rejecting or calling into question the Hebrew scriptures.

2. He did not see himself as undermining obedience to the will of God revealed in the law or as advocating antinomianism.

3. Paul's focus on obedience to the law deserves much more attention than it usually receives. . . . Paul would [not] have agreed that he had a negative view of the law.

4. Paul did not see himself as breaking with Judaism.

5. Whereas formerly the center of gravity or dominating force for Paul and other Jews was the law, now he found that center of gravity in Christ.

6. Turning to Christ is done in keeping with Old Testament faith, not in rejection of it.[37]

How does Paul's view of the purpose of the law fit with my proposal concerning the covenant? Paul speaks of the law as "increasing sin" (Gal. 3:22, 24; Rom. 5:20); as bringing wrath (Rom 4:15); as a means to find life (Rom. 7:10); and as giving knowledge of sin (Rom. 3:20).[38] I would contend that these are all functions of the law, predictable exigencies of its revelatory purpose. When God's holy character was revealed through the law, knowledge of sin, guilt, and a basis for punishment all resulted. These are important by-products, but they do not diminish the positive purpose of the law.

Paul's stand on the law can now also be seen as not at all inconsistent. Yet it is possible to accept that it is the covenantal nomism (as per Edward P. Sanders) of the Pharisees (understood as their *traditio*) that has been rejected as the key to God's plan for his people and as the normative interpretation of how a relationship with God is to be maintained.[39] Even beyond that, however, is the concept that the Mosaic foundation of law has been redefined in Christ. The new covenant has new stipulations, though they come as normative interpretation of the old and with the same basic concerns as the old. It is not wrong to adhere to the old law, but it is wrong to relate to God through the old covenant's stipulations. As we have discussed in the previous chapters, the people of God have been redefined in the new covenant, and it is no longer possible to relate to God on the old basis. James D. G. Dunn has posed the question that echoed through the first century and the Pauline epistles: "What difference does the coming of Jesus the Messiah make to our traditional understanding of the covenant?" He summarizes Paul's answer as follows:

> Paul's new answer is that the advent of Christ had introduced the time of fulfillment, including fulfillment of his purpose regarding the covenant. From the beginning, God's eschatological purpose in making the covenant had been the blessing of the nations: the gospel was already proclaimed when God promised Abraham, "In you shall all the nations of the earth be blessed." So, now that the time of fulfillment had come, the covenant should no longer be conceived in nationalistic or racial terms. No longer is it an exclusively Jewish *qua* Jewish privilege. The covenant is not thereby abandoned. Rather it is broadened out as God had originally intended—with the grace of God which it expressed separated from its national restriction and freely bestowed without respect to race or work, as it had been bestowed in the beginning.[40]

What does this mean for the Jewish people? Are they still bound by the law? For several reasons, I believe the answer is no. First, Christ has redefined the stipulations of the covenant. The spirit of the law has come to fruition in his life and ministry. Second, ethnic Israel can no longer be defined as the people of God, though believing Jews are part of the people of God on the criterion of faith. Relationship with God can only take place through the blood of Christ. Therefore circumcision is no longer of any value. Thirdly, the normative interpretation of the law is now to be found in the teaching of Christ. Adherence to the law, or more precisely, to the spirit of the law, is measured by a new standard. The old adherence is insufficient. As Dunn sees it, this was precisely the point Paul was making.

> It is precisely the degree to which Israel had come to regard the covenant and the law as coterminous with Israel, as Israel's special prerogative, wherein the problem lay. Paul's solution does not require him to deny the covenant, or indeed the law as God's law, but only the covenant and the law as "taken over" by Israel.[41]

Are Jews wrong to adhere to the law today? The answer depends on why they are doing it. If they are still seeking to live under the old agreement and relate to God as ethnic Israel of the old covenant, they are ignoring, and perhaps it could be said, denying, the work of Christ. On the other hand, if they see in the performance of law a means by which they can imitate and proclaim the holiness of God, who can object?

It is common today to see the division of the law into moral, civil, and ceremonial categories as originally proposed by Thomas Aquinas. As convenient as this may seem, the Bible knows of no such categories.

> The classic rationale for a distinction between commands which are not binding on the Christian, and other commands which are, is the division of OT laws into the moral, the civil, and the ceremonial. But this division is an unsatisfactory instrument for analyzing the laws. In one sense it is too blunt: there is a wider variety of law than this division indicates. In another sense, the division is too sharp an instrument, for moral, ceremonial and civil cannot be distinguished as sharply as it implies. Even Calvin, while accepting the division, notes that ceremonial and civil laws embody moral principles. While this may not be the case with circumcision, it is the case with the sabbath and with the payment of tithes.

It is easy for a distinction into moral, civil and ceremonial to lead to practical importance being attached only to the first category. We have seen already that in a carefree way the OT mingles various types of command, suggesting the view that all are to be seen as aspects of accepting the Lordship of the one Yahweh. All the commands of the OT are specific to their circumstances, all have to be seen in the light of Christ's coming, but all may be instructive today in the light of the principles they embody.[42]

In discussions concerning the validity of the law for Christians today it is common for interpreters to seek guidelines for determining what is of lasting value or relevance and what is not. Besides the threefold division mentioned above, others look to the New Testament for the criterion. Either all the law has continuing validity except that which is repealed in the New Testament, or none has except that which is specifically reiterated in the New Testament.[43] All, however, appear to be too stringent in their requirements. The law is written on our hearts by the indwelling Spirit of Christ. It is not comprehensively codified in text, though we must be guided by the written revelation that has been provided for us with the New Testament leading the way in how we should understand Old Testament law.

Rather than imposing artificial categories on the text, our model suggests that the entire law can retain its revelatory validity. That does not mean it has obligatory force. The obligation is inherent in the covenantal relationship as it has always been. In our time it is the covenantal relationship through Christ that helps us to apply the law appropriately so that its intended ends are achieved. I therefore agree with David Dorsey that "legally, none of the 613 stipulations of the Sinaitic covenant are binding upon NT Christians, including the so-called moral laws, while in a revelatory and pedagogical sense all 613 are binding upon us, including all the ceremonial and civic laws."[44] He further explains,

> A law reflects the mind, the personality, the priorities, the values, the likes and dislikes of the lawgiver. Each law issued by God to ancient Israel (like each declaration of God

through the prophets) reflects God's mind and ways and is therefore a theological treasure. Moreover the theological insights we gain from a particular OT law will not only enhance our knowledge and understanding of God but will also have important practical implications for our own lives if we are patterning them after our heavenly Father and modifying our behavior and thinking in response to our knowledge of him and his ways (Paul argues along these very lines in 1 Cor. 9:9–10). It is in this sense that every one of the 613 laws of Moses is binding upon the NT Christian.[45]

It is certainly unnecessary for the church (as it was for the early Gentile converts to Christianity) to feel any obligation to the law. The covenant in its Mosaic phase was made with the Jews and was never intended to be universal in scope. We are not expected to enter into an obsolete form of the covenant. The covenant law that has carried over as interpreted by Christ has validity to us as interpreted by Christ. It is the law of Christ to which we are obliged. Law cannot and must not be treated independently of its covenant context.[46]

Is there any reason for the Christian today to study the laws of the Pentateuch? Yes, but we must understand what we are about. The laws were given as examples of the implications of the holiness of God. We still have a mandate to understand the holiness of God. As God's revelation of himself and his character, the law still has much to offer us. To return to an earlier analogy, though a guide can get someone where they are going more efficiently and more expertly than a map can, a map can offer an understanding of the whole picture, give one a feel for the terrain, and provide an important sense of orientation. The law no longer provides a normative definition of how we ought to relate to God, and it has certainly become outdated as a description of the shape of society,[47] but it can still offer a clear understanding of the areas of life that should be affected by the holiness of God. If one is interested in knowing God, the law has much insight to offer.[48]

THE SOTERIC FUNCTION OF THE LAW

This has not been a book about salvation and how it has or has not been accomplished throughout the ages. In fact, I have come to the conclusion that it is the concern with soteriology (not inappropriate in itself) and the attempt to bring all of the text into dialogue with soteriological issues that has had some role in creating a good deal of confusion.[49] Instead of approaching the text with soteriological questions, the model that has been proposed in this book suggests that soteriological issues only arrive at the top of the theological agenda once God's plan of salvation has appeared on the horizon. This does not mean that soteriology had no previous importance, only that the revelatory process had not addressed the issue with sufficient clarity to bring it into prominence. It is important then to identify several of the ways in which the law did address some of the issues of soteriology.

The law served as a conceptual model for a number of soteric tasks prior to the coming of Christ. Atonement and justification could only be totally and finally accomplished by the work of Christ on the cross. But the sacrificial system provided a mechanism for the motions to be carried out (therefore affirming and laying the foundation for important theological concepts). Atonement is addressed by the substitutionary death of an animal. Justification is approximated by the act of *kipper* that, unfortunately, is often translated *atone*.[50] Regeneration is partially accomplished through the expected internalization of the law, whereas the new covenant speaks of the time when the law will be in the heart in a different way. I understand this as being fulfilled in the indwelling-regeneration function of the Holy Spirit. Finally, the law also provides the concept for sanctification in that it urges the people to be holy as God is holy. That is, the law supplies the details of how one could conform to the character of God.

All of these concepts existed in the law but no efficacious mechanism was provided. Therefore, sin reigned through the law. This is not a fault in the law, for the law was not intended to be a soteric mechanism, it was a revelatory instrument. So as the law taught us what God is like, it also taught us what sin is. But in Christ we are freed from that tyranny of the law—the tyranny that offered no option but to try to be like God through our own efforts. In the New Testament the soteric aspects are finally more achievable for we have Christ as our model and perfecter of our faith, and the Holy Spirit as the sanctifying and regenerating agent. We are then able to become godlike by being Christlike.

This brief statement certainly leaves many important questions unanswered. I maintain, however, that it is not the burden of the text to answer all of our soteriological questions. It is the intention of the text to reveal God. In trying to make it soteric throughout, we have done it a disservice. Identifying soteriology's appropriate place in exegesis and in the progress of revelation in no way minimizes the theological treasure of our personal salvation, nor does it trivialize its central importance to the gracious plan of God.

NOTES

[1]See a detailed comparison in H. J. Boecker, *Law and the Administration of Justice in the Old Testament and Ancient East* (Minneapolis: Augsburg, 1980); and John Walton, *Ancient Israelite Literature in its Cultural Context* (Grand Rapids: Zondervan, 1989), 69–92.

[2]Raymond Westbrook, "Cuneiform Law Codes and the Origins of Legislation" *ZA* 79 (1989): 201–22.

[3]Raymond Westbrook, *Studies in Biblical and Cuneiform Law* (Paris: Gabalda, 1988), 5.

[4]D. J. Wiseman, "Law and Order in the Old Testament" *Vox Evangelica* 8 (1973): 7. Shalom Paul, *Studies in the Book of the Covenant in the Light of Cuneiform and Biblical Law*, VT Supp. 18 (Leiden: Brill, 1970), 25.

[5]Moshe Greenberg, "Some Postulates of Biblical Criminal Law" in *Essential Papers on Israel and the Ancient Near East*, ed. F. Greenspahn (New York: New York University Press, 1991), 336; E. A. Speiser, "Cuneiform Law and the History of Civilization" *Proceedings of the American Philosophical Society* 107:6 (1963): 537; Shalom Paul, *Studies in the Book of the Covenant in the Light of Cuneiform and Biblical Law*, 6–7.

[6]This is substantiated by the studies that show that Deuteronomy organizes its legal material around the decalogue with the collections of laws serving as illustrations of implications of each of the ten commandments in order. See S. A. Kaufman, "The Structure of the Deuteronomic Law" *Maarav* 1/2

(1978-79): 105-58; and J. H. Walton, "Deuteronomy: An Exposition of the Spirit of the Law" *GTJ* 8 (1987): 213-25.

[7]Shalom Paul, *Studies in the Book of the Covenant in the Light of Cuneiform and Biblical Law*, 36-37.

[8]This purpose of the law enjoys widespread acceptance. In *The Law, the Gospel and the Modern Christian: Five Views*, edited Wayne Strickland (Grand Rapids: Zondervan, 1993), three of the five authors specifically support this concept and no one contests it. Willem VanGemeren speaks of Israel as a witness to the nations with the Lord "showing them in the law how to mirror his perfections" (p. 30). Strickland explicitly refers to the revelatory function when he asserts: "The revelatory function of the law was in mind when Paul discussed the merits of the law." He goes on to conclude that "the nature of the law has not changed, so its revelatory purpose transcends the Mosaic economy and remains valid in the church dispensation. In fact, the law as it functions in a revelatory manner acts to preserve the unity between the two eras. Since God's character is immutable, it stands to reason that insofar as the law reveals God's character, it remains valid" (p. 280). See also Moo's comments along the same lines, (p. 339).

[9]Dale Patrick, *Old Testament Law* (Atlanta: John Knox, 1985), 198-200; Michael Fishbane, *Biblical Interpretation in Ancient Israel* (Oxford: Clarendon Press, 1985), 91-95. A didactic function of the law is articulated in passages such as Deuteronomy 17:18-20; 31:9-13; and 2 Chronicles 17:7-9.

[10]See Anthony Phillips, *Ancient Israel's Criminal Law* (Oxford: Blackwell, 1970), 153. Behavioral obligation is not always determined by law. The stipulations of a treaty must be adhered to and must dictate behavior. They are not laid down by law, but they do carry obligatory force. To say that Old Testament law was not legislation per se does not weaken the obligation that it imposed on the people.

[11]Shalom Paul, *Studies in the Book of the Covenant in the Light of Cuneiform and Biblical Law*, 123-24.

[12]Thus the rabbinic dictum: "What is Torah? It is the exposition of Torah" see J. Weingreen, *From Bible to Mishna* (New York: Holmes and Meier, 1976).

[13]J. Weingreen, *From Bible to Mishna*, 150.

[14]Michael Fishbane, *Biblical Interpretation in Ancient Israel*, 272; Raymond Westbrook, *Studies in Biblical and Cuneiform Law*, 134-35; J. G. McConville, *Law and Theology in Deuteronomy* (Sheffield: JSOT Press, 1984): 154.

[15]Michael Fishbane, *Biblical Interpretation in Ancient Israel*, 96-97, 257. See also J. Weingreen, *From Bible to Mishna*, especially pages 143-53. Weingreen sees Deuteronomy as the first example of an "oral Torah" and therefore refers to it as a "proto-Mishna."

[16]Michael Fishbane, *Biblical Interpretation in Ancient Israel*, 276-77.

[17]Dale Patrick, *Old Testament Law*, 204. This is precisely the process that is behind the development of the Mishnah and is additionally evident in the work of Maimonides. See J. Weingreen, *From Bible to Mishna*, 143-44.

[18]B. S. Jackson, "The Ceremonial and the Judicial: Biblical Law as Sign and Symbol" *JSOT* 30 (1984): 33.

[19]Michael Fishbane, *Biblical Interpretation in Ancient Israel*, 276–77.

[20]J. Weingreen, *From Bible to Mishna*, 146.

[21]M. Jack Suggs, *Wisdom, Christology, and Law in Matthew's Gospel* (Cambridge: Harvard, 1970), 106–7, concluding his discussion of Matthew 11:28–30: "What we confront in Matthew is law opposed to law. The yoke of Jesus is not some other yoke than the yoke of the Torah. Rather, the yoke of the true Torah, of Wisdom, is set over against that of Pharisaic Torah—as the two Sabbath pericopes (Matt. 12) clearly show." (p. 107). Similar conclusions are drawn by T. McComiskey, *The Covenants of Promise* (Grand Rapids: Baker, 1985), 100.

[22]W. D. Davies, *Paul and Rabbinic Judaism* (Philadelphia: Fortress, 1970), 226; see also page 148–49. This is not to suggest that this new Torah was a written code of Christ's commands, a view refuted by H. Raisanen, *Paul and the Law* (Philadelphia: Fortress, 1983), 77–82.

[23]This illustration was suggested in a sermon by Dr. Perry Downs at South Park Church, Park Ridge, Ill., July, 1992.

[24]Stephen Westerholm, *Israel's Law and the Church's Faith* (Grand Rapids: Eerdmans, 1988), 203.

[25]Robin Nixon, "Fulfilling the Law: The Gospels and Acts" in *Law, Morality and the Bible*, ed. Bruce Kaye and Gordon Wenham (Downers Grove: InterVarsity Press, 1978), 69; see also Douglas Moo, "The Law of Moses or the Law of Christ" in *Continuity and Discontinuity: Perspectives on the Relationship Between the Old and New Testaments*, ed. John Feinberg (Wheaton: Crossway, 1988), 205; and Stephen Westerholm, *Israel's Law and the Church's Faith* (Grand Rapids: Eerdmans, 1988), 204.

[26]M. Jack Suggs, *Wisdom, Christology, and Law in Matthew's Gospel*, 114.

[27]This element is directly related to the new covenant as observed by M. Weinfeld, "While Jeremiah speaks of *putting the law within them*, Ezekiel speaks of *putting the spirit within them* (36:27), for the law remains as before and only the spirit of man changes." Weinfeld, "Jeremiah and Spiritual Metamorphosis" *ZAW* 88 (1976): 32. Among the most helpful studies of Matthew 5:17–19 are Robert Guelich, *The Sermon on the Mount* (Waco: Word, 1982), 138–42; Douglas J. Moo, "The Law of Moses or the Law of Christ" in *Continuity and Discontinuity*, 203–6; and D. A. Carson, "Matthew" in *The Expositor's Bible Commentary*, vol. 8, ed. F. Gaebelein (Grand Rapids: Zondervan, 1984), 140–47. It is not within the purview of this book to treat exegetically all of the New Testament passages regarding the law. In-depth discussion of the exegetical issues can conveniently be found in the recent book *The Law, the Gospel and the Modern Christian: Five Views*.

[28]J. M. G. Barclay, "Paul and the Law: Observations on Some Recent Debates" *Themelios* 12.1 (1986): 12.

[29]The clearest summary of the various solutions that I have come across is in Klyne Snodgrass, "Spheres of Influence: A Possible Solution to the Problem of Paul and the Law" *JSNT* 32 (1988): 94–96.

[30]N. T. Wright, *The Climax of the Covenant* (Minneapolis: Fortress, 1991), 241. The title of the book is Wright's rendering of the phrase *telos nomou* in Romans 10:4. Compare the similar remarks of D. K. Lowery: "In its day, the law was a glorious phenomenon, the focus of God's revelatory self-disclosure to humankind. But the focus has changed. It has moved on or progressed to Christ, to what he has said and done." "Christ, the End of the Law in Romans 10:4" in *Dispensationalism, Israel and the Church*, ed. C. A. Blaising and D. L. Bock (Grand Rapids: Zondervan, 1992), 239. These conclusions are basically in agreement with the analysis of R. Badenas, *Christ the End of the Law* (Sheffield: JSOT Press, 1985), see especially 79–80 for summary.

[31]For a helpful discussion of the different interpretations of the "works of the law" that cannot justify, see Thomas Schreiner's remarks in G. F. Hawthorne et al., *Dictionary of Paul and His Letters* (Downers Grove, Ill.: InterVarsity Press, 1993), 975–79.

[32]N. T. Wright, *The Climax of the Covenant*, 192. For defense of the concept that this coincided with common concepts in ancient Judaism see F. Thielman, *From Plight to Solution* (Leiden: Brill, 1989).

[33]For an expression of this consensus see H. Raisanen, *Paul and the Law*, 16, though Raisanen himself believes that Paul is operating with a double concept of law without noticing it (p. 21). For a good summary of the discussion see Thomas Schreiner, *The Law and Its Fulfilment* (Grand Rapids: Baker, 1993), 33–40.

[34]This *traditio* can be understood as coinciding with E. P. Sanders' covenantal nomism (without accepting Sanders' understanding of Paul) and can be viewed in terms of J. D. G. Dunn's identity and boundary markers. The former sees obedience to the law as the means of maintaining the covenant relationship; see *Paul and Palestinian Judaism* (Minneapolis: Fortress, 1977) and *Paul, the Law, and the Jewish People* (Minneapolis: Fortress, 1983). The latter maintains that "the recognition that what Paul is attacking is a particular and restrictive understanding of the law provides the key to many of the tensions perceived in Paul's writing on the law. Freed from that too-narrow understanding of the law, the Jewish Christian (and Gentile) is able to recognize that the law has a continuing positive role, to be fulfilled in love of neighbor" (J. D. G. Dunn, *Jesus, Paul and the Law* [Louisville: Westminster/John Knox: 1990], 231).

[35]Klyne Snodgrass, "Spheres of Influence: A Possible Solution to the Problem of Paul and the Law," 95. To draw a distinction between the *traditio* of the Pharisees and the New Torah that is Christ is not to suggest that the former was a perverted misuse of the law nor to be equated with legalism as Cranfield proposes.

[36]This is discussed widely in the literature. For a basic treatment see D. Moo in *The Law, the Gospel and the Modern Christian: Five Views*, 362 and the

documentation accompanying that article. For discusion of "works of the law" see Schreiner, 41–71, and also his discussion of legalism, 93–121.

[37]Klyne Snodgrass, "Spheres of Influence: A Possible Solution to the Problem of Paul and the Law," 96–97. His solution to the controversy is also attractive, but treatment of it here would take us too far afield.

[38]Sanders, *Paul, the Law, and the Jewish People*, 70. See Schreiner, *The Law and Its Fulfillment*, 87–88.

[39]A survey and analysis of this literature would take us far beyond the scope of this study. The following works will introduce the reader to the issues: J. M. G. Barclay, "Paul and the Law: Observations on Some Recent Debates," 5–15; W. D. Davies, *Paul and Rabbinic Judaism*; J. D. G. Dunn, *Romans 1–8* (Waco: Word, 1988), lxiii–lxxii; and *Jesus, Paul and the Law*; Douglas J. Moo, " 'Law,' 'Works of the Law,' and Legalism in Paul" *WTJ* 45 (1983): 73–100; and "The Law of Moses or the Law of Christ" in *Continuity and Discontinuity*, 203–18; E. P. Sanders, *Paul and Palestinian Judaism*; and *Paul, the Law, and the Jewish People*; Peter Tomson, *Paul and the Jewish Law* (Minneapolis: Fortress, 1991); Stephen Westerholm, *Israel's Law and the Church's Faith*; Schreiner, *The Law and Its Fulfillment*.

[40]James D. G. Dunn, *Jesus, Paul and the Law*, 197. This is expressed by Paul in Eph. 2:11–12.

[41]Ibid., 202.

[42]John Goldingay, *Approaches to Old Testament Interpretation*, (Downers Grove: InterVarsity Press, 1981), 64–65. See also the excellent treatment by David Dorsey, "The Law of Moses and the Christian: A Compromise" *JETS* 34 (1991): 329–32. For a demonstration of how difficult it is to maintain this distinction in Paul see H. Raisanen, *Paul and the Law*, 23–25.

[43]For all of these variations see *The Law, the Gospel and the Modern Christian: Five Views*.

[44]David Dorsey, "The Law of Moses and the Christian: A Compromise" *JETS* 34 (1991): 325. Though the number 613 is the result of the classification by Maimonides, it is used here as a reference to the entire law of Moses.

[45]Ibid., 332.

[46]See W. J. Dumbrell, "The Prospect of Unconditionality in the Sinaitic Covenant" in *Israel's Apostasy and Restoration*, ed. A. Gileadi (Grand Rapids: Baker, 1988), 143.

[47]See the excellent presentation by David Dorsey, "The Law of Moses and the Christian: A Compromise," 325–29.

[48]For some hermeneutical guidelines for this process see David Dorsey, Ibid., 332–33.

[49]It is interesting to note that H. Raisanen sees this specifically as the problem that also created confusion in Paul, *Paul and the Law*, 154. While I would not be inclined to see Paul as being confused by this matter, I am of the opinion that Paul's need to address the law in terms of its soteric functions has led to much of the confusion that persists today.

[50]The recent literature on *kipper* is substantial. A few of the more significant studies may be listed here: Herbert Chanan Brichto, "On Slaughter, Blood and Atonement" *HUCA* 47 (1976): 19–55; Marilyn Katz, "Problems of Sacrifice in Ancient Cultures" in *The Bible in Light of Cuneiform Literature, Scripture in Context III*, ed. W. W. Hallo, B. Jones, and G. L. Mattingly (Lewiston, N.Y.: Mellen Press, 1990), 117–41; N. Kiuchi, *Purification Offering in the Priestly Literature* (Sheffield: JSOT Press, 1987), 87-109; Baruch Levine, *In the Presence of the Lord* (Leiden: Brill, 1974), 55–77; 123–27; Jacob Milgrom, *Leviticus 1–16* (Garden City, N.Y.: Doubleday, 1991), 1079–84.

11

SUMMARY AND CONCLUSIONS

The findings and hypothesis of this book can best be summarized by addressing the question, "What is new about this perspective?" The most basic difference among it and others was stated in chapter 1: That while the covenant is characteristically redemptive (i.e., God's redemptive attributes are part of what is being revealed), formulated along the lines of ancient treaties, and ultimately soteric (i.e., eventuating in a program of salvation), it is essentially revelatory. This depar-ture provides a basis for reevaluating every aspect of the covenant along with its connected theology and constructs. The implications concern primarily the continuity-discontinuity of the covenant(s), the conditionality of the covenant(s), and our understanding of the people of God.

CONTINUITY-DISCONTINUITY

The emphasis of this proposal has been on the continuity of the covenant under the umbrella of its revelatory purpose. The phases (Abrahamic, Mosaic, and Davidic) are linked together in a developmental pattern. Although each makes a distinctive contribution to the program of revelation, they should not be viewed as featuring discontinuity. The greatest discontinuity comes with the new covenant. This phase in-cludes a roll over into the soteric program, thus qualifying as a separate category within the overall scheme. Nevertheless, its

179

role within the revelatory program, its elements of election and revelation, and its inclusion of the previous covenant factors all represent the continuity that it enjoys with the other phases.

In this category the hypothesis under discussion resembles covenant theology more than classic dispensationalism, though progressive dispensationalism is not very distant. Covenant theology, on the other hand, while agreeing with the continuity here promoted, combines all of this under the redemptive-soteric structure of the covenant of grace—an altogether different understanding.

CONDITIONALITY-UNCONDITIONALITY

As a result of our study in the concept of covenant jeopardy, and in light of the revelatory purpose of the covenant, we have concluded above that the essential nature of the covenant, in each of its phases, is unconditional. That is, the decision of God to reveal himself within the confines of the covenant was neither subject to reconsideration nor vulnerable to abrogation. Yet, the program of revelation was not designed to be forever unfolding. Despite the fact that the program itself has come to a conclusion, the effects of it continue to exist and always will. The Davidic throne will ever be occupied by its proper and legitimate heir, Jesus, the Christ; the law will always stand as testimony to the holy character of God; the history of Israel will forever bear witness to God's sovereign kingship. The conditions that exist in each phase have been identified within a framework of covenant jeopardy that offered some new categories for understanding to which sort of jeopardy those conditions related. This perspective blends in a unique way what have historically been the concerns of covenant theology and dispensationalism.

THE PEOPLE OF GOD

The approach taken toward the people of God is that Israel was the elect people of God in a revelatory sense, while the new covenant introduces a soteric definition of the people of God that then applies to all believers, Jew or Gentile. This differs from the classic covenant theology, which sees all believers of all ages as the people of God, in that it suggests that in the old covenant the term *people of God* was not a soteric classification. Terms like *the elect* and *people of God* should not be given exclusively soteric definitions, for they are not exclusively soteric categories. We have no argument with covenant theologians that the "saved" of all ages stand as a unified group.

This understanding of the people of God also differs from dispensationalism's view in that it accepts the concept of a unified people of God in the church age rather than maintaining ethnic Israel as a separate people of God. Israel has ceased to be the revelatory people of God, though those who accept the new soteric definition are included in the soteric people of God. Agreement with dispensationalism can be found in the understanding that Israel remains an identifiable subgroup of the soteric people of God on the basis that they may still have a material inheritance based on their previous function as the revelatory people of God. Against covenant theology, I disagree that the church has replaced Israel; but against dispensationalism, I also disagree that ethnic Israel retains its place as the people of God. The people of God has been redefined and believing Gentiles have joined with believing Israel in the new configuration. The church has not replaced Israel because the revelatory role Israel played is no longer necessary.

CAN EVERYONE BE RIGHT?

By proposing a new solution to these problems it is not my intention to suggest that everyone else has been wrong. The revelatory aspect of the covenant has always been recognized, but it has never been put in this place before. When it is given the position suggested here, the possibility exists that many scholars on both sides of the discussion have been mostly on target. This new proposal draws heavily on the research and theological concerns of so many who have gone before. To suggest that the position I have presented is "right" is at best premature and more likely abjectly presumptuous; likewise, to say that everyone is right is to trivialize significant controversies. But to consider that there may be a position that incorporates the main contributions of all sides and offers

ISSUE	COVENANT THEOLOGY	CLASSICAL DISPENSATIONALISM*
Pattern of History	Covenant of Works with Adam; Covenant of Grace with Christ on behalf of the elect (some distinguish between covenant of Redemption with Christ and covenant of Grace with the elect).	Divided into dispensations (usually seven); e.g., Innocence (pre-fall), Conscience (Adam), Human Government (Noah), Promise (Abraham), Law (Moses), Grace (Christ's First Coming), Kingdom (Christ's Second Coming).
God's Purpose in History	There is a unified redemptive purpose.	There are two distinct purposes, one earthly (Israel), one heavenly (church).
View of Biblical Covenants	They are different administrations of the Covenant of Grace. Temporal promises are conditional and applicable to the church.	They mark off periods of time during which God's specific demands of people differ. Temporal promises are unconditional and are applicable to ethnic Israel.
Relationship of OT Law to NT	Acceptance of Old Testament teaching required unless specifically abrogated by New Testament.	Old Testament prescriptions are not binding unless reaffirmed in the New Testament.
Relationship between Israel and the Church	The church is spiritual Israel, in continuity with true Israel of the Old Testament.	The church is the spiritual people of God, distinct from Israel, the physical people of God.
OT Prophecy	Refers to God's people, the church.	Refers to ethnic Israel.
Church Age	God's redemptive purpose continued to unfold.	There is a parenthesis between past and future manifestations of the kingdom.

Columns 1 and 2 adapted from R. C. Walton, *Chronological and Background Charts of Church History* (Grand Rapids: Zondervan, 1985) 65. Column 3 provided by Darrell Bock and used with permission.

*This position attempts to merge the positions held by the early dispensationalists

THEOLOGICAL SYSTEMS

PROGRESSIVE DISPENSATIONALISM	"REVELATORY" VIEW
Divided into dispensations, of which four are prominent: Patriarchal (Promise); Mosaic (Law); Ecclesial (Church); Zionic (Millennium, the New Heavens and New Earth).	Revelation and election initiatives succeeded by human failure to respond appropriately. Periods of transition then lead to further initiatives.
To manifest his glory in a progressive redemption that covers every sphere of creation and every structure of human relationship.	The objective of self-revelation is pursued culminating in the revelation of a plan of salvation, whereby the goal of relationship may be achieved. It is a unified purpose, but not soteric throughout.
The biblical covenants of promise (Abrahamic, Davidic and New) are made originally to His people, Israel. Believing gentiles are included through Christ, who is the means of blessing for all who believe. All covenants have an "already-not yet" structure.	There are revelatory initiatives facilitated through various types of election. Temporal promises are conditional but remain applicable to ethnic Israel. The covenant is characteristically redemptive; ultimately soteric; but essentially revelatory.
Individual aspects of the Law are assessed canonically on a case-by-case basis. Christ fulfills and completes the law.	Old Testament legal passages function within the covenant serving a revelatory purpose that continues to be relevant. The law of Christ has been superimposed on the law of Moses.
Church: the unified community that receives God's spiritual blessings in Christ. Israel: the national and political community in the midst of the nations that ultimately will be blessed fully by God. Ultimately united in redemption.	The church is the people of God defined soteriologically. Israel, previously the revelatory people of God, now may cross over and become a subset of the soteriological people of God (now that their revelatory function is complete) if they respond by faith to the plan of salvation.
Fullness of blessing to be given to believing Israel (and those in the nations who believe) in the final dispensation.	Refers to ethnic Israel but conditional upon their faithful response.
From Pentecost to rapture, a phase in the progressive outworking of God's wholistic redemption. It is not a parenthesis in the kingdom program.	The period begun when the people of God are defined soteriologically as a result of God's plan of salvation being revealed.

such as Scofield and Chafer, with the next generation represented by Ryrie and Walvoord. It should be recognized that there were differences between these generations in the articulation of dispensationalism.

compromise on issues of less substance certainly would not constitute mitigation of one's ideals or disrespect toward one's heritage.

CONCLUDING PRACTICAL APPLICATION

If the above thesis is true, it is evident that we need to revolutionize our handling of the Old Testament in our pulpits, Bible studies, and curricula. We can no longer justify treating the narration of history as a repository for spiritual role models. When we do this, we often focus on the soteric element (e.g., was Saul "saved"?) and study the Bible for revelation concerning the spiritual condition of its characters. We need to turn our attention again to the revelation that the Bible offers us of God. In that way we will remain true to the authoritative teaching of the text.[1] For example, it is common to study Abraham, Moses, or David as models of spirituality. We analyze in great depth the Bible's biographical information and its accounts of their activities looking for clues to a successful relationship with God. Often there is at least a tacit assumption that the Old Testament exists to provide exactly that sort of information. Therein lies the fallacy. Whatever the nature of the relationship to God that these individuals enjoyed, their stories are not recorded to offer models of what our relationship to God should or should not be. Rather, the Old Testament accounts seek to reveal what God is like so we may enter into relationship with him. Knowing Abraham, Moses, or David does not provide the key to a successful relationship with God—knowing *God* provides the key to a successful relationship with God. Understanding the covenant as a program of revelation can help us to keep our focus when studying the Old Testament.

NOTES

[1]For a more detailed treatment of this issue, particularly for curriculum, see J. Walton, L. Bailey, and C. Williford, "Bible-based Curricula and the Crisis of Scriptural Authority" *Christian Education Journal* 13/3 (1993): 83–94.

SCRIPTURE INDEX

AUTHOR INDEX

SUBJECT INDEX